A History of
CHINA

'In Brief': Books for Busy People

by Anne Davison

Copyright2019 Anne Davison

Cover Design by Karen Turner

OTHER BOOKS BY THE SAME AUTHOR

A History of Russia

Abraham's Children: Jew, Christian, Muslim; Commonality and Conflict

From the Medes to the Mullahs: a History of Iran

Making Sense of Militant Islam

Paul of Tarsus: a First Century Radical

The Holy Roman Empire: Power Politics Papacy

The Mughal Empire

The Ottoman Empire

*****

http://www.inbriefbooks.com

CONTENTS

MAPS

PREFACE

Napoleon Bonaparte, when referring to China, famously said; *"China is a sleeping giant. Let her sleep, for when she wakes, she will shake the world."* His words were prophetic. For centuries China slumbered. Then, about forty years ago she woke up and since that time has risen to become the world's second largest economy by GDP, with the world's greatest purchasing power.

This book tells the story of China's long history. To attempt this in under 200 pages is admittedly ambitious. But this is the aim. In common with other titles in the 'In Brief' series, the book is written for the general reader who does not have the time, or inclination, to read a heavy academic tome. It gives an overview of China's complex history in an accessible and informative style, with maps, charts and timelines to help the reader navigate through the text.

Starting with the pre-historical Yellow Emperor, the earlier chapters trace China's major dynasties, including the Han, Tang and Ming. Twice during its long history, the country was ruled by non-Chinese dynasties: the Mongol Yuan between the 13th and 14th Centuries and the Manchu Qing, the last of the imperial dynasties, that ruled between the 17th and 20th Centuries. The later chapters cover the decline and fall of the Qing, the Republican era and finally Communist China.

Writing any history book is heavily dependent upon available sources. There are very few written records for the earlier period and they are not necessarily reliable. Very often the manuscripts have been written decades after the events occurred. Also, scholars have argued that facts have been inserted into the original text, perhaps for political reasons. This was particularly true during the earlier centuries of Imperial China when court historians were commissioned to write an 'official' history that generally portrayed the commissioning Emperor in a favourable light compared to the preceding ruler.

Unfortunately, some of the early written records of China's history have been lost or destroyed. In about 200 BC, the first Emperor of the Qin Dynasty is said to have ordered the burning of 'undesirable' books and as late as the Cultural Revolution, between 1966 and 1976, certain historical books were banned and often destroyed.

An added disadvantage for this particular author is that while there is a wealth of material written for the Chinese reader, very little of the early material has been translated into English. However, with modern technology, we now have tools other than the written word. For example, with the help of drones and special cameras, we now have other tools for discovering the past. Of course, what we see, often on our television screens, is still open to interpretation by the 'experts', be they guides, academics or TV presenters.

Today we are overwhelmed with information. This presents a different challenge. We have to sift through vast amounts of material, much of which may be suspect. In today's world of 'fake news', much of this may well be 'fake history'.

In writing this book, my aim has been to use reliable sources wherever possible. Equally I hope that I have pointed out the need for a critical reading. For clarification, I have used BC and AD for the first two chapters. Thereafter, AD has been dropped unless needed.

An added confusion can arise with place names. For example, today's Beijing was known as Khanbaliq in the Mongol Yuan period (1271-1368) and Peking at the time of the Qing (1644-1912). And today's Xi'an was known as Chang'an during the Tang Dynasty (618-907).

While there will inevitably be gaps in a work of this size, it is hoped that the reader may be inspired to further reading on the subject. For those interested, a short selection of the main works that have been consulted is provided at the back.

Finally, I would like to thank those friends and colleagues who have given of their time to read through various chapters, to proof read the script, as well as to offer helpful comments.

*****

CHAPTER ONE
Ancient Period: 2698-256 BC

China, with thousands of years of continuous history, is one of the oldest civilisations in the world and is regarded as a cradle of civilisation. A well-known example of its early habitation is the discovery in 1923 of skeletal bones and stone tools near Beijing. These remains are estimated to be between 680,000 and 780,000 years old. In 1923, at the time of the discovery, Beijing was known as Peking, hence the find became known as Peking Man.

Carbon dating provides evidence of rice cultivation in the Yangtze River region as far back as 8,000 years and cliff carvings from the same period show scenes of hunting and fishing as well as a possible form of early writing. Archaeologists have also discovered remains of buildings and pottery along the Yellow River basin, which suggests that settlements existed as far back as 5,000 BC.

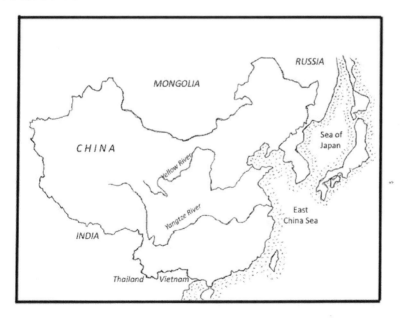

Ancient Texts

The first written records of Chinese history date back to around 300 BC in the form of chronicles that were recorded on bamboo or wooden panels. These panels were then bound together in bundles of about thirty. The best-known texts are the *Bamboo Annals* and the *Records of the Grand Historian.*

Although the *Bamboo Annals* were not written until around 300 BC, the author starts his history many centuries earlier with the legendary Yellow Emperor, who was said to have ruled between 2698 and 2598 BC. Since there were no written records going back so far, the author relied on oral folklore and myth. Consequently, the line between fact and fiction for this early period of history is blurred.

The *Bamboo Annals* relate the history of dynasties and events up to 299 BC, which was during the time of the Zhou Dynasty. The original text was buried with King Xiang of Wei in 296 BC. Over five centuries later, in 279AD, fragments of the *Annals* were discovered after a robber broke into the King's tomb.

Today there are two versions of the *Annals*: an 'ancient text' that has been pieced together from the original text, and a 'current text' that was compiled in the 16th Century. Since that time, there has been ongoing debate regarding the authenticity of the 'current text'. The majority view tends towards the reliability of the earlier version over the 'current text'.

The *Records of the Grand Historian,* also known as *Shiji,* was started around 150 BC by Sima Tan, who was Court Astrologer and historian at the time of the Western Han Dynasty (206 BC-9AD). The work was completed in 94 BC by his son, Sima Qian. In common with the *Annals,* the *Records* start with the Yellow Emperor, but the manuscript covers a longer period, going up to the reign of Emperor Wu (141-87 BC).

The manuscript, which was longer than the Old Testament, was gathered into about 600 bamboo bundles. Consequently, they were heavy, making their circulation difficult. Writing on silk was possible at the time, but it was expensive. It was around this time that the Chinese began experimenting in the papermaking process and would eventually lead the way in the manufacture of paper.

The *Records* comprised 130 chapters, divided into five sections. Topics included accounts of the ancient rulers and dynasties, genealogical tables and treaties on ritual, music, astronomy, waterways and financial administration.

As Court Historians, both Sima Qian and his father had access to vast libraries. Qian also travelled extensively, asking ordinary people about their lives, experiences and especially memories of past events. A feature of ancient Chinese history is that the authors did not aim to provide an uninterrupted chronology. Rather, historians wrote about separate dynasties and events as distinct units. Consequently, there was a degree of overlap.

The earliest extant version of the *Records*, which was handwritten, dates back to around 450. Two copies have survived, both of which are held in libraries in Japan. Later versions were block printed and included commentaries.

The *Records* is considered to be the foundational text of Chinese history and has been in almost continuous publication since its inception. A recent version was published by the Zhonghua Book Company in Beijing, a company that specialises in the *Twenty-Four Histories*, which are China's official historical books.

The Yellow Emperor: c 2697-2597 BC

Sima Qian, author of the *Records*, began his chronicle with the period of the Yellow Emperor, also known as the Yellow Thearch, or Yellow God. His Chinese name is *Huang di* and he is said to have lived from 2697 BC to 2597 BC. Given these dates, it is not surprising that there has been ongoing debate over his historicity.

According to Chinese tradition, the Yellow Emperor was among the group of ancient deities, or god-kings, known as 'The Three Sovereigns and Five Emperors'.

The role of the Three Sovereigns was to care for the people and promote their welfare, education and training. It is claimed that the Sovereigns taught the people how to use fire, to build houses and farm land. They introduced medicine, the calendar and writing. The Yellow Emperor's wife is said to have introduced the production of silk.

The five Emperors, also referred to as the Five Deities, were five different manifestations of the one supreme god of heaven who resided in the North Celestial Pole. Each Deity was associated with a different colour, season, mineral and planet.

	BLACK DEITY Winter, water Mercury	
WHITE DEITY Autumn, metal Venus	YELLOW DEITY (Yellow Emperor) Saturn	BLUEGREEN DEITY Spring, wood Jupiter
	RED DEITY Summer, fire Mars	

The Yellow Emperor was associated with the colour yellow and his planet was Saturn. Unlike the other Emperors, the Yellow Emperor did not represent a particular season. In Chinese theology, he holds the central position. He is said to have been the initiator of Chinese civilisation and crucially, the ancestor of the Han Chinese people.

Throughout most of early Chinese history, the Yellow Emperor was believed to have been a historical person. In common with divine figures of other cultures, he had a miraculous birth. According to tradition, his mother conceived after being hit by a bolt of lightning from the celestial Big Dipper.

During the 1920s, a group of academics known as the 'Doubting Antiquity School' questioned the historicity of the Yellow Emperor. The scholars were critical of all the ancient histories that were based on folklore and myth. In the case of the Yellow Emperor, the 1920s scholars postulated that he was originally a god who was later historicised.

Whatever the truth may be regarding the origins of the Yellow Emperor, his significance in Chinese culture has been profound. Towards the end of the Qing Dynasty (1644-1911), when China was facing instability and looking to rediscover her glorious past, the Yellow Emperor once more became a powerful national symbol.

With the collapse of the Qing Dynasty the Cult of the Yellow Emperor was suppressed by the new Republican Government. However, following the death of Mao Zedong in 1976, the ancient Emperor/Deity was once more reinstated as the cultural ancestor of the Chinese people.

Battle of Banquan c 2500 BC

According to Sima Qian, author of the *Records of the Grand Historian,* *(Shiji),* a great battle took place between the Yellow Emperor *(Huang di)* of the Youxiong Tribe and the Flame Emperor *(Yan di),* of the Shennong Tribe.

Considered to be the first battle in Chinese history, both the location and date has been disputed. Most historians, however, have placed the battle in the 26th Century BC and the likely location being a plateau west of the Taihang Mountains, a range that runs from north to south through today's Shanxi, Henan and Hebei provinces.

The Yellow Emperor defeated the forces of the Flame Emperor, who sued for peace. The Shennong and Youxiong Tribes then amalgamated and became known as the Hanhuang Tribe. Led by the Yellow Emperor, this new alliance began a process of expansion, incorporating surrounding towns and villages into Hanhuang territory.

The alliance of the Shennong and Youxiong under the Yellow Emperor marked the beginning of the Huaxia civilisation. To this day, the Chinese people refer to themselves as 'descendants of Yan and Huang'.

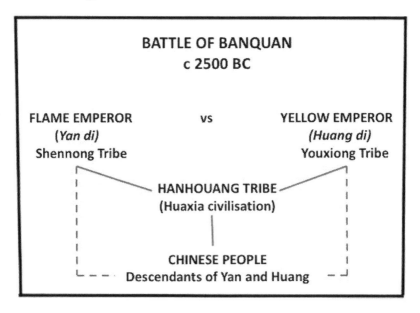

The Great Flood

According to the *Records*, another event of significance in ancient Chinese history, was the Great Flood, which is thought to have occurred in the 3rd millennium BC, during the reign of Emperor Yao (2333-2234 BC).

The flood is said to have lasted for two generations and resulted in vast devastation, mass migration and famine. Faced with the enormity of the disaster, Emperor Yao decided to appoint an official to be responsible for controlling the flood.

On the recommendation of his advisers, known as the Four Mountains, he appointed a distant relative named Gun, Prince of Chong. Gun, like Yao, was a descendent of the Yellow Emperor.

According to tradition, Gun spent nine years building dams and embankments in an attempt to hold the waters back. But despite the fact that he used a magical form of self-expanding soil, the floods continued unabated.

In the face of continual flooding, social disorder broke out. Emperor Yao lost control of the people and once more appealed to the Four Mountains. He was told to appoint Shun, who was another distant relative and descendent of the Yellow Emperor. Shun proceeded to reorganise the empire and reassert imperial authority. He created nine islands, each island having a 'sacred mountain'. The 'sacred mountain' became the capital of each island and the islands were to become the forerunners of today's provinces.

Shun then toured around the entire empire, standardising rules and regulations as well as weights and measures. His innovations proved to be so successful that Emperor Yao appointed Shun as his successor.

For all Gun's efforts, he never did control the floods. The task then fell to his son, Yu, who adopted a different approach. Rather than building dams to stop the water, Yu dredged the rivers and dug canals in order to facilitate drainage. According to tradition, he employed different tribes to dig the canals and he was also helped by various mythological characters such as a yellow dragon and black turtle. It is also said that the god of the Yellow River provided Yu with a map of the waterways.

Historians have long debated the historicity of the flood and the stories around Gun and Yu. However, in 2016, a group of international scientists published a paper that supported the theory that a massive flood did indeed occur in the Yellow and Yangtze River valleys in around 1920 BC.

The study was led by Qinglong Wu of the China Earthquake Administration's Institute of Geology in Beijing, and it took almost ten years to complete. The authors concluded that if the flood was a historical fact, then the deeds of Gun and Yu could contain an element of truth. Even if Gun and Yu were mythical characters, they were probably based upon a historical leader who was capable of bringing order out of chaos.

The story of the flood, and how the Chinese people survived it, is a central theme in Chinese culture, mythology and poetry. It is also crucial in understanding how the first dynasty in Chinese history, the Xia dynasty, came to be founded.

THE FIVE EMPERORS/DEITIES

Yellow	*mythological*
Zhuanxu	*mythological*
Ku	*mythological*
Yao	2333-2234 BC?
Shun	2233-2184 BC?

THE FIRST DYNASTIES

Xia (Yu the Great)	2070-1600 BC?
Shang	1600-1046 BC
Zhou	1046-256 BC

The Xia Dynasty: c 2070-1600 BC

The author of the *Bamboo Annals* placed the Xia Dynasty around 1989-1558 BC. However, since this was centuries before written records and there was no archaeological evidence for the Xia, some believe the Dynasty to be purely mythical.

Historians have suggested a possible link between the Xia and the Erlitou culture that existed in the Yellow River valley at the same period. However, although archaeologists found evidence of palace buildings and particularly bronze vessels dating from this time, there are no inscriptions that mention the Xia.

Consequently, in 1996, the Chinese Government commissioned a team of experts to investigate the historicity of the Xia as well as the two successive Dynasties; the Shang and the Zhou. Known as the Xia-Shang-Zhou Chronology Project, some 200 scientists and academics worked on radiocarbon dating, textual analysis of historical documents and other methods, such as astronomical data.

The aim of the Project was to ascertain, as far as possible, an accurate dating and location for the first three Chinese Dynasties. The experts concluded that the most likely date for the Xia Dynasty was 2070-1600 BC.

According to tradition, Yu was the founder of the Xia Dynasty. It is said that Emperor Shun was so impressed with Yu's success in controlling the flood, that he named Yu, rather than his own son, as his successor.

Yu is referred to as King, rather than Emperor, of the Xia. Once in power, he was able to capitalise on his previous work. In the process of controlling the flood, he had established an efficient irrigation system. This naturally led to increased food production and therefore increased wealth. Consequently, Yu was able to expand his territory by incorporating surrounding towns and villages.

Towards the end of his life, rather than selecting the most capable person to succeed him, as had been the practice in the past, Yu nominated his son, Qi. This was to be the beginning of dynastic rule in China that was to last until the end of the Qing dynasty in 1912.

Yu is celebrated in Chinese history as the ideal philosopher king, earning the epithet 'the Great'. This was not to be the case with Jia, the 17th and last ruler of the Xia, who is believed to have reigned between 1789 and 1758 BC.

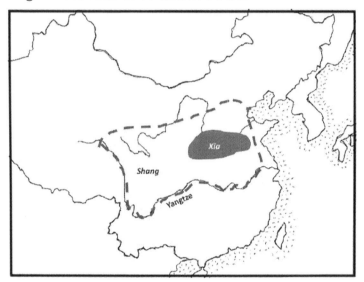

Shang (Yin) Dynasty: 1600-1046 BC

Jia, the last of the Xia Kings, was considered a cruel despot who lived a life of decadence. Being more interested in wine and women, he neglected his duties towards the people. It was only a matter of time therefore, before he faced an uprising from his subjects.

The challenge came from Tang, who ruled the Shang Kingdom which was a vassal state of the Xia. Tang took advantage of Jia's unpopularity. He formed an army that included forces from other disaffected Kingdoms and defeated Jia's forces at the legendary Battle of Mingtiao. Jia fled the scene and Tang became the first ruler of the Shang Dynasty, which is also referred to as the Yin Dynasty.

As with the earlier empires and dynasties, we get most of our information about the Shang from the *Bamboo Annals* and *Records of the Grand Historian,* as well as the *Book of Documents,* which was another classic text of ancient China. The Shang period was also studied by the 1996 Chronology Project, which placed the Dynasty between 1600 and 1046 BC.

However, unlike the previous Dynasties, we do have archaeological evidence that supports the historicity of the Shang. In 1928, the remains of royal tombs and palaces were discovered in a small village close to today's Anyang city in Henan Province. The find included weapons, jade artefacts, hair combs, oracle bones and bronze vessels with inscriptions that referred to the Shang kings and their capital cities.

In the 1950s, remains of a fortified settlement were discovered in Zhengzhou, also in Henan Province. The surrounding walls are estimated to have been up to 26 feet high, stretching some four miles in diameter around the settlement.

The archaeological evidence shows that the Shang had a developed form of writing and a sophisticated religious and court life. The kings performed priestly duties alongside their secular duties and evidence shows that animal, as well has human, sacrifice was widespread.

Excavation of palace tombs revealed remains of humans, horses, eating and drinking vessels being buried alongside a King. This suggests that the Shang had a strong belief in an afterlife.

According to the various chronicles, and from what can be gleaned from the contemporary inscriptions, seventeen Kings ruled during the Shang period, which lasted about 550 years. The last King, Di Xin, appears to have been even more despotic than Jia, the last king of the previous Dynasty. In common with his predecessor, he preferred wine and women to the business of state.

According to tradition, Di Xin was intelligent and handsome. At the beginning of his reign he was considered a good ruler, but he soon came under the influence of his wife Daji, who although beautiful, was said to be possessed by an evil fox spirit.

Daji encouraged Di Xin into a life of excess and debauchery. They built a lake in the palace grounds and filled it with wine. In the centre was an island of trees, on the branches of which hung roast meat. As they sailed round the lake in a small boat, they drank the wine from cups and when hungry they ate the meat from the overhanging branches.

Another form of entertainment, that caused them great excitement, was watching their subjects suffer the most brutal form of torture. All this is reminiscent of the debauchery of some Roman Emperors, particularly Nero and Caligula.

In order to pay for their lavish lifestyle, Di Xin imposed heavy taxation on the people who were already suffering due to his incompetent rule. Rebellion was inevitable, once the right leader came forward.

This time the challenge came from the vassal Kingdom of Zhou in the West of the Kingdom. King Wu of Zhou commissioned one of his noblemen, Jiang Ziya, to depose Di Xin and in 1046 BC, the Zhou troops defeated the Shang at the Battle of Muye. Faced with defeat, Di Xin gathered all his treasures around him. He adorned his body with all his jewels and then burned himself to death.

The Zhou Dynasty: 1046-256 BC

The defeat of the Shang signalled the rise of the Zhou, which was to be the longest dynasty in Chinese history, lasting some eight hundred years. The Zhou period is divided into two phases: the Western Zhou, from 1046 to 771 BC, and the Eastern Zhou from 771 to 256 BC. The transition reflected a change in the orbit of power from Western to Eastern China.

Wu, the first King of Zhou, died shortly after defeating the Shang. He was succeeded by the young and inexperienced King Cheng, but the real power was in the hands of Cheng's uncle the Duke of Zhou. When rival claimants attempted to seize the throne from Cheng, the Duke of Zhou not only put down the rebellions, but he also succeeded in expanding Zhou territory.

It is in this context that the doctrine of the 'Mandate of Heaven' came to be formulated as a way of legitimising the sovereignty of a king or emperor. According to the doctrine, Heaven, or the Will of the Universe, granted a mandate to a just ruler. If a ruler was overthrown, it was a sign that Heaven was displeased and had therefore withdrawn the Mandate.

Natural disasters were also a sign that Heaven had withdrawn its mandate. Consequently, the people often took such disasters as justification for rebellion against a ruler.

The Mandate of Heaven further permitted the overthrow of an unjust or despotic ruler. This was how the Zhou came to justify the overthrow of the Shang and it was a principle that remained in place throughout imperial China.

When the Zhou defeated the Shang, they gained extra territory which was divided into hereditary fiefs that were given to junior members of the dynasty. The system was somewhat similar to European medieval feudalism. In theory, the fiefdoms were vassal states of the Zhou King but in time some vassals became almost as powerful as the King.

By 771 BC, King You was in a weak position compared to some of the more powerful fiefdoms. When he died it was decided to move the capital further East to the city of Wancheng. This marked the beginning of the Eastern Zhou period.

Throughout the following three centuries, royal authority continued to decline, while the vassal states became more powerful and increasingly independent. The period is known as the 'Spring and Autumn period', taking its name from the contemporary *Spring and Autumn Annals.*

With no central authority, conflict became the norm between the different states, as each vied for power. This instability, known as the 'Waring States Period', continued until 256 BC, when the Zhou Dynasty was succeeded by the Qin Dynasty.

Hundred Schools of Thought

As often happens in times of instability and the breakdown of society, people begin to look elsewhere for moral authority and leadership. It is at these times that the arts, culture, literature and religion may bring meaning into people's lives.

In the case of China, the instability of the 'Waring States Period', in the latter half of the Zhou Dynasty, led to a Golden Age in Chinese philosophy known as the 'Hundred Schools of Thought'. The name reflects the hundreds of different philosophical ideas that were circulating at the time. The best known of these are probably Confucianism and Taoism.

Confucius, whose Chinese name was *Kong Fuzi,* meaning 'Master Kong', was born in about 551 BC, in the city of Qufu, close to the Eastern coast of China. Although he came from a middle-class background, he was raised in poverty due to his father's early death. Despite this, his mother managed to send the boy to school, albeit one for commoners.

After holding various government positions, Confucius embarked upon a series of long journeys expounding his philosophical theories. During this time of instability, it was common for advisers to lose their Government positions and become itinerant scholars acting as advisers to the many different state rulers.

We get most of our information about Confucian thought from the *Analects,* which are said to be a collection of the philosopher's sayings that were written shortly after his lifetime.

Central to his philosophy was the concept of relationship; both earth's relationship with heaven, and individual human relationships.

Confucius placed a strong emphasis on the family, which he stressed was the basis of society. He taught that wives should respect their husbands and children respect and obey their parents. In terms of Government, he said 'Let the ruler be a ruler and the subject a subject'. He believed that provided a person lived in accordance with his or her defined social status, and performed their duty accordingly, then peace and prosperity would prevail.

One of Confucius' greatest sayings, that is as relevant today as it was 2,500 years ago, was "Do not do to others what you do not want done to yourself", otherwise known as the 'Golden Rule'. It is a 'rule' that has been incorporated into the teachings of all the main world Faiths.

Taoism was another important philosophic school. It was founded by Laozi, a semi-mythical figure, thought to be a contemporary of Confucius. Stressing the importance of living in harmony with the Tao, or 'Way', Taoism emphasises the importance of maintaining a balance with the natural world rather than follow strict ritualism as propounded by Confucius.

Apart from these two major philosophical schools, there were many others, for example, the Legalists who were attached to the Ministry of Justice and Agriculturists. Their role was to advise the Ministry of Agriculture.

In the absence of a strong central authority, different segments of society designed their own guidelines for living. Some of these schools were short-lived. Others merged into new schools. However, Confucianism, and to a lesser extent Taoism, has survived to the present day, not just in China, but across the world.

Conclusion

In order to understand Chinese culture, an awareness of ancient Chinese history, which goes back some 5,000 years, is essential. Semi-mythical Emperor/Deities, such as the Yellow Emperor, heroes of ancient battles and the story of the Great Flood, are all embedded in the Chinese sense of identity.

We get most of our information about this early period from the *Bamboo Annals* and the *Records of the Grand Historian.* The difficulty is that this history was written by court historians, such as Sima Qian, long after the events are said to have occurred. Consequently, their historicity has frequently been open to question, particularly during the early 20th Century at the time of the 'Doubting Antiquity School'.

An indication of the importance of ancient history for the Chinese today, is the commissioning of various academic studies that attempt to verify the historicity of the early dynasties, as well as locate them in time and place.

One of the best-known studies is the 'Xia-Shang-Zhou Chronological Project' conducted by the People's Republic of China in 1996. While the results of the study have been accepted by some scholars, others are critical of both the methodology and conclusions.

It is generally accepted, however, that while questions remain regarding the Xia and Shang dynasties, we can be far more confident regarding the latter period of the Zhou, since by that time, inscriptions referring to the Zhou rulers have been found on bronze vessels.

Recent studies have also provided evidence that a Great Flood did indeed occur in the Yellow and Yangtze River Valleys, but a few decades later than traditionally thought. In this context, it is interesting to note that other cultures, particularly in the Mesopotamian region, also hold a belief in a great flood.

Another theme that is common to both ancient Chinese and Judeo-Christian cultures is the concept of the female temptress:

Daji in the Chinese tradition and Eve in the Judeo-Christian tradition.

The flood in Chinese history is remembered not just in terms of a national disaster, but for the heroic efforts of those who tried to fight it. The legacy of the flood was the introduction of a drainage and canal system that enabled the country to develop its agriculture and therefore grow in wealth and power.

The latter period of the Zhou Dynasty, known as Eastern Zhou, was a period of fragmentation. As royal influence declined, feudal kingdoms emerged, each vying for power. A product of the resulting instability was a flourishing in art, literature and above all philosophy. It was a 'golden period' of openness and tolerance, but one that could not last.

*****

CHAPTER TWO

Early Dynasties: 221 BC – 220 AD

The Qin Dynasty: 221–206 BC

During the Warring States Period of the latter part of the Zhou Dynasty, numerous feudal kingdoms battled for supremacy. Eventually, due to their more advanced administration and military skills, seven states emerged as the main contenders.

In 361 BC, Duke Xiao, ruler of the Qin, which was one of the larger of the seven states, introduced a policy of Legalism in his territory. According to this school of thought, human nature was inherently selfish. Social order could only be maintained by imposing strict discipline from above, which was enforced through a code of Law including harsh punishments. It was a policy that would later support two thousand years of imperialistic rule and it was a policy that enabled the Qin to conquer all the other states.

Between the rule of Duke Xiao in 361 BC and the reign of King Ying Zheng, who came to the throne at the age of 13 in 247 BC, the Qin Dynasty progressively annexed all other six states. The first state to fall, in 230 BC, was the Han. The last, in 221 BC, was the Qi.

In 220 BC, having unified all opposing states, King Ying Zheng assumed the title 'Shi Huang di', meaning First Emperor. 'Shi' signified 'first', 'Huang' referred to the 'Three Sovereigns' and 'di', the Five Emperors, and specifically the Yellow Emperor.

By assuming such a title, Ying Zheng was claiming direct descent from the ancient semi-divine, 'Three Sovereigns and Five Emperors'. (See Chapter One) Consequently, Ying Zheng became the founder of the Qin Empire, which was to be the first Empire in Chinese history. He is more popularly referred to as Emperor Qin.

Consolidation

Ying Zheng (now Emperor Qin) was assisted throughout the period of conquest by Li Si, who had been his Chancellor, or Prime Minister, since 247 BC. Li Si was a Legalist and an able politician. He now put these skills into consolidating the new Empire.

The first task facing Emperor Qin and his chancellor was to impose uniformity across the disparate states that formed the new Empire. He unified the weights and measures system as well as the currency and alphabet. He introduced uniform widths for roads and canals as well as imposing a common gauge for carriage wheels.

In order to eradicate the power of the previous rulers of the Warring States Period, Emperor Qin abolished feudalism, replacing it with a system based on meritocracy.

One of the greatest changes, however, was the imposition of Legalism on the population, together with the abolition of all other schools of thought, such as Confucianism and Taoism, that had been part of the 'Hundred Schools of Thought'. (See Chapter One) The justification for this decision was that such philosophies would be incompatible with the official policy of Legalism.

Li Si then feared that the leaders of the deposed schools could become a focus for dissent. His solution was to encourage Emperor Qin to invite the most able scholars from the conquered states to join the imperial administration. Those who refused to do so, were viewed as a threat and they were conveniently 'disposed' of, probably by assassination.

Burning of the Books and Burying of Scholars

Throughout history and within all cultures, literature has been subject to censorship. The written word can be a powerful tool for dissent and those in power understandably monitor both what is being written and perhaps more importantly, what is being read.

In 220 BC, the nascent Chinese Empire was no exception. According to tradition, within a few years of coming to power, Emperor Qin ordered the burning of all texts relating to poetry, philosophy and especially history. Apart from Legalism, the only texts of the 'Hundred Schools of Thought' that were exempt, were those relating to agriculture, medicine and divination. Books on divination survived because they provided essential guidelines for communicating with the ancestors, which was a central part of Chinese culture at the time.

Despite the order to burn such valuable books, Emperor Qin ordered that two copies of all texts, including those to be destroyed, should be placed for safe keeping in the Imperial library. It is believed that these copies were later destroyed during the fighting at the fall of the Qin dynasty. The *Bamboo Annals*, referred to in the previous Chapter, survived the burning because they had been buried with King Xiang of Wei in 296 BC and not discovered until 281 AD.

According to Sima Qian, author of the *Shiji*, or *Records of the Grand Historian*, soon after the burning of the valuable works, Emperor Qin ordered the burying alive of some 460 Confucian scholars because he believed that he had been tricked by two alchemists, thought to be Confucians. In order to discover the culprits:

The first emperor therefore directed the imperial censor to investigate the scholars one by one. The scholars accused each other, and so the emperor personally determined their fate. More than 460 of them were buried alive at Xianyang, and the event was announced to all under heaven for warning followers. (*Shiji*, chapter 6)

According to Sima Qian, the Emperor's son, Fusu, attempted to intervene, pointing out that the execution of so many Confucian scholars could lead to unrest. The advice was ignored and Fusu was sent as punishment to guard the frontier, which meant virtual exile

Throughout the Imperial period of China's history, the martyrdom of the Confucian scholars was never questioned. However, since the fall of the last Empire in 1912, historians have looked back at China's Imperial past with a more critical eye and in recent years, some have questioned the reliability of Sima Qian's accounts.

Ulrich Neininger, in his article *Burying the Scholars Alive: On the Origin of a Confucian Martyrs' Legend*, (June 2012) claims that both stories were possibly added to the texts at a later date in order to portray Emperor Qin as a cruel despot. Proof that the previous ruler was corrupt would legitimize his overthrow in line with the removal of the 'Mandate of Heaven' from the offender and passed to a just ruler.

Neininger supports his view on the grounds that contemporary records made no mention of either the burning of the books or the burying of the scholars. Rather, both events first appeared in the *Records of the Grand Historian*, which was written by Sima

Qian (c 146-80 BC), over a hundred years later, during the succeeding Han dynasty. Sima Qian was a court historian and his task would have been to portray the Han in a favourable light compared to the Qin.

Today's historians also point out that many of the books that were supposedly burned on the orders of Emperor Qin, were frequently quoted in later centuries by scholars. This would suggest that the texts continued to be in circulation, rather than being totally destroyed.

The consensus seems to be that stories of Emperor Qin's cruelty and despotism have probably been exaggerated for political reasons. At the same time, it is most probable that some destruction of books and execution of scholars did indeed occur, but not on the scale as traditionally believed.

The Great Wall

During the Warring States Period, the various rulers erected walls and fortifications to protect themselves against other states. When Emperor Qin came to power his aim was to unify all these states under his rule. He therefore ordered that all internal fortifications should be pulled down.

Of greater concern, was the north west frontier which was open to barbarian invasions from the Xiongnu people of Mongolia and the Gobi Desert. So he embarked upon an ambitious programme to build a wall along the northern frontier linking up any previous fortifications that had been built as protection against the Xiongnu.

Until recently, the length of Great Wall was unknown. Today, with the help of modern scientific methods and particularly the use of drones, it has been possible to establish that it could have measured some 21,000 kilometres in length, stretching from the North Korean border, deep into the Gobi Desert.

It is also evident that there were originally many walls, all made of rammed earth. Extra fortifications were built along the length of the walls and a coded system of flags and bonfires warned of an imminent Xiongnu invasion

The wall that we see today was largely built during the Ming Dynasty between 1368 and 1644. (see Chapter Five) It is made of large bricks with a white coloured mortar which was thought to be made of the crushed bones of slaves who had died building the wall. It is now known that the mortar was actually made from a substance using sticky rice and it has proven to be effective over many centuries.

During the Ming period, the wall was intended as a barrier to keep nomadic Mongol tribes out. Today it is part of China's new 'Silk Road Project' and the local guides will tell you that it symbolises a bridge, rather than a barrier, to the rest of the world.

The Terracotta Army

According to tradition, Emperor Qin was obsessed with death and finding the secret to longevity and everlasting life. Soon after coming to the throne he started to plan his mausoleum that would also contain everything he would need for his after-life.

In 1974, some local farmers in the Lintong District of Xi'an, dug up some pieces of pottery that turned out to be fragments of the terracotta army that had guarded Emperor Qin in his tomb.

Scientists have subsequently concluded that the mausoleum was part of a much larger necropolis covering an area of some 38 square miles. While the mausoleum itself, which contains the tomb, has yet to be excavated, scientists have concentrated on four main pits, each about 23 feet deep.

The first pit, which is divided into corridors, contains the main army of some 6,000 terracotta warriors. Other pits contain high ranking officers, horses and war chariots. Smaller excavations have revealed thousands of fragments of bronze vessels, together with swords and daggers that are marked with inscriptions.

All the warriors are life size and were originally brightly painted. Great effort went into making them look life-like. For example, rather than all the faces being identical, on close examination, each face is different. It is also possible to determine the rank of each warrior from the detail in their clothing. For example, generals, middle-ranking officers and the infantry could each be identified according to their headdress, belts and insignia on their uniforms.

There is still much to be excavated on this huge site, but what has been revealed to date gives a valuable insight into the structure of the military and type of warfare in China at the time of the Qin Empire.

End of the Qin Dynasty

Emperor Qin died in September 210 BC. He had consumed a concoction of mercury that was intended to extend his life. Instead, it killed him.

At the time of his death, the Emperor was away from his capital of Xi'an. The journey back would take two months. Li Si, his Prime Minister, was travelling with him, and he decided to keep the death secret until their arrival in the capital.

Throughout the journey, the corpse was given a change of clothing and even offered food, while the face was kept hidden. When the body started to decompose, Li Si arranged for carts of rotting fish to travel in front, and behind, the Emperor's carriage in the hope of concealing the foul smell of the corpse.

This practice of concealing the death of a ruler has been common in many cultures throughout history. The Ottomans, for example, sometimes concealed the death of a Sultan until it was politically expedient to make a public announcement.

The natural heir to Emperor Qin Shi Huang was his eldest son, Fusu. According to Sima Qian, Fusu had been sent to the frontier as punishment for challenging his father over the execution of the scholars. But Li Si and his close followers were opposed to

Fusu and they devised a way of tricking the heir to the throne into committing suicide.

Li Si then succeeded in bringing the youngest son, Huhai, to the throne as Emperor Qin Er Shi. He was eighteenth in line of succession. Being young and inexperienced, he became a puppet ruler in the hands of Li Si and the chief eunuch, Zhao Gao. The result was a corrupt and cruel government which paved the way towards rebellion.

By 206 BC, just four years after the death of Emperor Qin Shi Huang, the Qin Dynasty fell to the Han.

The Han Dynasty: 202 BC – 220 AD

Qin Shi Huang had succeeded in founding the Qin Empire by annexing six of the major States at the end of the Warring States Period. However, the Qin Dynasty only lasted from 221 BC to 206 BC. During this relatively short period, rulers of the defeated States continued to harbour ambitions of regaining their independence.

When the Qin Empire went into decline after the death of Qin Shi Huang, Liu Bang of the Chu State and Xiang Yu of the Qin State, fought each other in a bid to take over the beleaguered Qin Empire. In the ensuing conflict, Liu Bang became King of the State of Han. At the Battle of Gaixia, Liu Bang defeated his rival, Xiang Yu, and he then went on to conquer the failing Qin Empire. In 202 BC, Liu Bang became the founder of the Han Dynasty with the title Emperor Gaozu of Han.

Emperor Gaozu came from a peasant background. At an early age he showed signs of strength, with an independent and rebellious streak. He was also extremely charismatic. According to Chinese legend, his mother conceived him while she was sheltering from a rainstorm. When his father went looking for her, he saw a dragon hovering over his wife's body. His mother was impregnated by the dragon and consequently it is believed that Emperor Gaozu descended from both Emperor Yao and through Yao, the Yellow Emperor.

Early in his reign, Emperor Gaozu reduced taxation and abolished the corvée system of forced labour. He also created vassal states by awarding princes and kings with land in return for military service.

In an attempt to secure peace with the Xiongnu, which continued to be a threat from the North, he introduced the system of *heqin*, which was a form of political marriage alliance. In common with ruling dynasties in other cultures, Chinese Emperors would marry off a junior princess of the royal family to a neighbouring power in order to cement a political alliance.

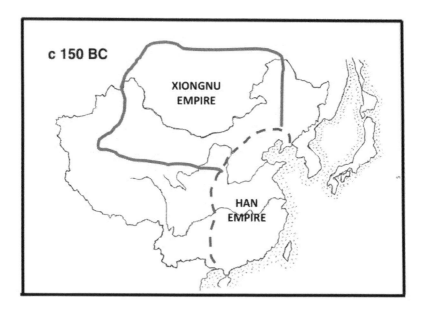

Probably one of the most important, and lasting, of Emperor Gaozu's early policies was to reintroduce Confucianism, which had been suppressed during the Qin Dynasty. From this point on, Confucianism would become the philosophical foundation of

Chinese culture. Legalism, however, remained as the means by which law was enforced. Consequently, a combination of Confucianism and Legalism would continue to influence later Chinese thought and practice.

Towards the end of his life, Emperor Gaozu openly displayed his favouritism for Concubine Qi over his wife, the Empress Lu Zhi. Even worse, he expressed a wish that Concubine Qi's son, Liu Ruyi, should succeed him rather than the crown prince Liu Ying.

This naturally led to hostility and court intrigue. Eventually, the Emperor was persuaded to give up the idea and the Crown Prince Ying, son of the Empress, assumed the throne as Emperor Hui.

One reason that Emperor Gaozu did not want Liu Ying to ascend the throne was because he had a weak character. This quickly became evident once he became Emperor. Throughout his short reign of seven years, Emperor Hui was dominated by his mother the Dowager Empress, who was the true power behind the throne.

Shortly after the accession of her son, the Dowager Empress Lu took her revenge on Concubine Qi and her son Liu Ruyi. According to the *Records of the Grand Historian*, she had Liu Ruyi poisoned and then:

'*she had Concubine Qi's limbs chopped off, blinded her by gouging out her eyes, cut off her tongue and locked her in the pigsty*'.

Emperor Hui was sickened by these acts but had been unable to stop his mother. From then on, he gave up all efforts to rule and turned to drink and drugs. This would not be the last time in Chinese history that the Dowager Empress would hold such power, and it would not always be for the good.

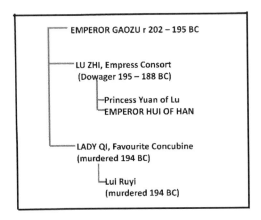

EMPEROR GAOZU r 202 – 195 BC

LU ZHI, Empress Consort
(Dowager 195 – 188 BC)

Princess Yuan of Lu
EMPEROR HUI OF HAN

LADY QI, Favourite Concubine
(murdered 194 BC)

Lui Ruyi
(murdered 194 BC)

Expansion

Apart from a short period under the Xin (9-23 AD), the Han Dynasty lasted for over four hundred years. The majority of Chinese people today identify themselves as Han Chinese and use a Han script.

The Han period is considered a golden age in China's long history. It was contemporary with two other great empires; the Roman Empire in the West and the Parthian Empire that straddled Central Asia.

Emperor Wu (141–87 BC) was probably the most popular of the Han Emperors. He ascended the throne at the age of 15 with high ideals and plans for reform. However, his reform programme was thwarted by the Grand Dowager and Dowager Empresses. It was only after the death of the Grand Dowager that he was able to implement his plans.

Under Emperor Wu, territory was gained in the South as far as today's Vietnam and in the North into the Korean Peninsula. He continued the policy of *heqin*, or marriage alliance, which helped to incorporate large parts of Central Asia and Mongolia into the Empire as vassal states. Consequently, the Han Empire came to border the Parthian Empire, which in turn bordered the Roman Empire. Roman coins and pieces of Parthian pottery have been discovered in China that provide evidence of trade between the three great powers.

The relative stability of these three neighbouring Empires allowed for the development of the Silk Road that stretched from the Mediterranean Sea to China. It was the West's desire for precious Chinese silk that gave the Silk Road its name.

The opening of the Silk Road brought great wealth to all cities along its route and also led to an improvement in the economy of China. As well as trade, ideas also travelled along the route between East and West. Consequently, China's scientific and technological innovations, as well as philosophical ideas, spread to the West.

Since that time, there have been moments in history when the road has become inaccessible, largely due to war. However, today China is embarking upon an ambitious project to revitalise the Silk Road, not only along its traditional, ancient route, but also southwards through Vietnam, Cambodia and Myanmar.

Innovation

It was during the Han Dynasty that some of China's greatest innovations took place. One of the best known is the manufacture of paper. Although hemp was used as wrapping paper in China as early as the 8th Century BC, it was during the Han Dynasty that paper for writing was first produced.

Around 105 AD, Cai Lun, an official of the Han court, is credited with the invention, using a combination of plant fibres, fishnets, old rags and hemp waste. By the 3rd Century AD the paper was being used for writing and by the 6th Century AD the Chinese were using toilet paper.

Other innovations included the invention of the ship's rudder, astronomical equipment and a seismometer used for measuring earthquakes. It is also said that the Chinese were the first to make use of negative numbers in mathematical calculations.

Imperial Music Bureau

Emperor Wu was known to be interested in all aspects of Chinese culture, particularly music, poetry and classical dance. Although music and poetry had been celebrated in China from pre-historic times, Emperor Wu raised the profile of these arts by founding the Imperial Music Bureau.

He brought together poets, musicians and dancers from across the Empire and under the auspices of the Bureau, a particular Han style of classical performing arts was created. The Emperor often commissioned works that included religious ritual, which was an integral part of the music and poetry.

The Imperial Music Bureau continued throughout much of the Imperial period but it was at its height under Emperor Wu of the Han Dynasty.

Decline of the Han Dynasty

After centuries of growth and prosperity, by around 189 AD, the Han Empire went into a period of decline that ended in its demise in 220 AD. This was largely due to a loss of central power, the rise of warlords and a major rebellion known as the 'Yellow Turban Rebellion'.

Throughout much of Imperial China's history, tensions existed between different interest groups, namely the different clans of the Dowager Empresses and Concubines, the Court Eunuchs, the Court Ministers and finally the small circle of advisers surrounding the Emperor himself.

Things came to a head during the reign of Emperor Ling (156-189). Known by the personal name of Liu Hong, he was chosen at the age of 12 to succeed Emperor Huan, who had no son. Since he was a minor, his mother, the Lady Dou Miao, who became Dowager Empress on her son's accession, acted as Regent. She was supported by her father, Dou Wu and the Confucian scholar Chen Fan.

The Palace Eunuchs opposed Emperor Ling's accession and a bitter conflict broke out between them and the Empress Dowager and her supporters. The Eunuchs succeeded in gaining control and they had the Dowager Empress placed under house arrest where she remained for the rest of her life.

On reaching adulthood, Emperor Ling showed no interest in State affairs, preferring to indulge in a life of debauchery. Consequently, corruption became widespread and heavy taxes were imposed upon the people. This left the Empire weak and vulnerable to power-seeking warlords.

Yellow Turban Rebellion and Taoism

The Yellow Turban Rebellion, also known as the Yellow Scarves Rebellion, was a peasant uprising that started in 184 AD, towards the end of the reign of Emperor Ling. It took its name from the yellow headgear worn by the rebels. Although the initial uprising was put down within a year, fighting continued for another 21 years.

The rebellion started following a period of famine and a series of minor floods which forced farmers and former soldiers to migrate Southwards. With an influx of labour from the North, landowners in the South were able to exploit the peasants by reducing their pay.

A major reason for the tenacity of the rebels was the fact that they were supported by Taoist groups and their leaders.

Taoism, meaning 'Teaching of the Way', had been a strong influence in China for many centuries. Its founder was Laozi, a semi-mythical philosopher/teacher said to be a contemporary of Confucius (551-479 BC). Another view is that he lived later, sometime during the Warring States period (475-221 BC).

One tradition claims that Laozi travelled to India where he met, and taught, the Buddha. Scholars have long debated the possible date, and route, for the arrival of Buddhism in China. The current thinking is that it took an overland route from India, through

Afghanistan and arrived during the Han period. Whatever the truth may be, it is evident that the Indian and Chinese religions share similarities, particularly regarding views on cosmology.

Another example is the similarity between the Taoist 'Three Pure Ones' and the Hindu 'Trimurti' (Brahma, Vishnu and Shiva). Both are trinitarian expressions of creation in the form of three gods. The Taoist text *Tao Te Ching* teaches that the "Tao produced One: One produced Two: Two produced Three: Three produced All Things."

This is remarkedly similar to the Christian Trinity, whereby the First Person (Father) produced the Second Person (Son). Opinions differ in Christian thought as to 'procession' of the Third Person (Holy Spirit), but all three somehow play a part in Creation.

Interestingly, while there is consensus among Taoists regarding the role of Pure One and Pure Two, scholars have long debated how Pure Two can produce Pure Three. Christians refer to the Third Person of the Trinity as the Holy Spirit. Taoists refer to the third Pure One as the *Chi*, or life force. In both cases the 'Spirit', or 'life force' would appear to be illusive.

Since Hinduism predates both Buddhism and Taoism, it is likely that Hindu thought influenced both Buddhism and Taoism. The link between the Taoist Trinity and Christian Trinity is less easy to explain, but not impossible. As mentioned earlier, ideas as well as trade travelled along the Silk Road. During the 4th Century AD some of these traders would have been Greek merchants who may well have been Christian. This was a period when the Church Councils were involved in a heated debate about the nature of the Trinity. It was a time when many Greeks argued passionately about the doctrine of the Church and they may well have carried their passion along the Silk Road.

By the time of the Han dynasty, Taoism had evolved into an influential and organised religious tradition with its own temples and priests. Correct ritual, that was so central to

Confucianism, took second place to following 'The Way'. Taoists placed the emphasis on living in harmony with nature and the cosmos in accordance with the *I Ching*, an ancient classic text.

A key Taoist doctrine was the importance of *yin-yang*, symbolising perfect balance in a duality of opposites, e.g. hot/cold, male/female and black/white. Black and white, placed within a circle, is the symbol of Taoism.

Imbalance destroyed harmony and would lead to sickness in an individual. Wars and natural disasters at communal level were a sign of imbalance and signified that the Mandate of Heaven had been withdrawn from the ruler.

The Three Kingdoms

When Emperor Ling died in 189 AD, he was succeeded by his eight-year old son, Liu Xie, known as Emperor Xian. But Liu Xie was Emperor in name only. In reality, he was the puppet of Dong Zhuo, a military general and warlord who had seized control in the on-going chaos of the Yellow Turban Rebellion.

In 220 AD, Emperor Xian was forced to abdicate the throne in favour of warlord Cao Pi. This marked the end of the Han Dynasty and the beginning of the 'Three Kingdoms' period which was one of the bloodiest periods in Chinese history.

Over a period of some sixty years, China was divided into three 'kingdoms': the Wei, the Shu and the Wu. Each state was ruled by a self-styled Emperor/warlord and the three warlords fought each other for sovereignty over a united China.

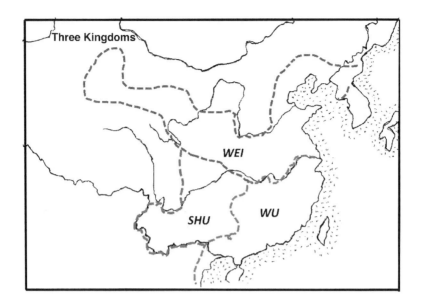

The story of the Three Kingdoms provides the background to the 14th Century classic novel *Romance of the Three Kingdoms.* It has also been depicted in TV series and provided material for video games. One of its most popular portrayals is the 2008 action-film *Three Kingdoms: Resurrection of the Dragon,* directed by Daniel Lee. The film is based on historical characters and is an authentic portrayal military warfare of the time.

Conclusion

The foundation of the first Qin Empire, in 220 BC, marked a watershed in early Chinese history. During his reign, the first Emperor, Shi Huang di, also known as Emperor Qin, unified weights, measures, currency and the alphabet. He also introduced standard widths for roads, canals and a common gauge for carriage wheels.

It was under Emperor Qin that the first phase of the Great Wall was built and he has also left his legacy in the immortalised form of his terracotta army.

Despite these innovations, as well as bringing a period of peace and stability to China, Emperor Qin has gone down in Chinese history as a cruel and despotic ruler. The justification for this accusation is based on the story of the 'Burning of the Books and Burying of the Scholars'.

However, modern historians have cast some doubt over the accuracy of these accounts. They point out that the first mention of the events, does not appear until much later, in Sima Qian's *Records of the Grand Historian*. At that time, both Sima Qian and his father held the post of Court Historian to the Han Emperor. Consequently, it was quite likely that Sima Qian was fulfilling the Emperor's wishes by portraying the previous Emperor in an unfavourable light, thereby justifying his overthrow according to the Mandate of Heaven.

Emperor Qin achieved a great deal in his short reign of approximately ten years. This was partly due to his imposition of Legalism with its authoritarian style of government, in favour of Confucianism. But as so often happened in Chinese history, his death signalled a period of instability which eventually led to the rise of the Han Dynasty.

The Han Dynasty, which lasted for around 400 years, is considered a golden age. Confucianism was reintroduced as the State philosophy while Legalism remained a tool of Government. This combination was to remain the foundation of Chinese culture for many centuries.

Under one of its most popular Emperors, Wu, the Han gained territory in today's Vietnam and the Korean Peninsula. Through the policy of *heqin,* or political marriage alliance, large parts of Central Asia were also annexed.

The acquisition of new territory in the West led to the development of the Silk Road, which opened up trade with both the Parthian and Roman Empires. At the same time the trade route facilitated the spread of ideas between East and West.

The Han period is also renowned for its many innovative achievements, one of the most famous being the invention of paper. It was also a high period for music and literature with the founding of the Imperial Music Bureau and commissioning of historical works such as that of Sima Qian.

After 400 years, its downfall was inevitable. It was triggered, as was so often the case, by the succession of a minor. This always resulted in conflict between rival parties, as each competed for power. In the case of the Han, famine and flood added to the political instability which in turn led to the Yellow Turban Rebellion.

Although the initial rebellion was put down, it survived in various forms for a further twenty-one years. This was largely because it was supported by Taoists, who by that time were well organised and had significant influence over the peasants.

As Imperial power decreased, the warlords moved into the power gap. The outcome was the creation of three separate kingdoms. For sixty years the Three Kingdoms were in bitter conflict as each fought to become the successor to the Han.

*****

CHAPTER THREE

The Tang: 618-907 AD

Between the fall of the Han Dynasty in 220 and the rise of the Tang Dynasty in 618, several short-lived dynasties, such as the Jin (220-420), the Liu Song (420-469), the Liang (502-557) and the Sui (581-618), attempted to rule a united China. However, they were usually thwarted by constant civil war in the North which was largely caused by a steady influx of non-Chinese tribes migrating across the Northern border from the Xiongnu and Xianbei regions. Two Dynasties of this period are worth mentioning: the Jin and the Sui.

The Jin Dynasty: 265 – 420

Sima Yan, the founder of the Jin Dynasty, rose to power by conquering the 'Three Kingdoms': the Shu in 263, the Wei in 266 and the Wu in 280. (see Chapter Two) Taking the name Wu of Jin, he then became Emperor of a united China.

MAJOR CHINESE EMPIRES	
Qin	220 BC – 206 BC
Han	206 BC – 220 AD
Jin	265 AD – 420 AD
Sui	581 AD – 618 AD
Tang	618 AD – 907 AD
Song	960 AD - 1279 AD
Yuan	1271 AD – 1368 AD
Ming	1368 AD – 1644 AD
Qing	1644 AD – 1912 AD

Prior to becoming Emperor, Wu had been an extremely capable leader, particularly on the battlefield. However, as Emperor he was said to be too soft and he was especially criticised for being over generous. He gave away land and concessions to his male relatives and favourite generals. As a result, he undermined his own authority, while his fiefdoms became increasingly powerful.

Emperor Wu also had a reputation for enjoying the company of women. According to tradition, he had 10,000 concubines and devised various methods to help him decide who should have the privilege of sharing his bed for the night.

When Emperor Wu died in 290, he was succeeded by his son, Emperor Hui, who was physically and mentally disabled. This led to a succession crisis. Conflict broke out between the clan of Wu's wife, Empress Jia, and his male relatives, many of whom had been able to build up personal armies as a result of the Emperor's earlier generosity.

Barbarian invasions and migration

For several centuries, Mongolic, Turkic and Tibetan nomadic tribes, had been migrating across the Northern border. At the time of the Jin Dynasty, the Xiongnu, Xianbei, Di, Qiang and Jie, known collectively as the 'Five Barbarians' had settled in Northern China.

During times of stability, the tribes lived peacefully with the ethnic Chinese and eventually many minority ethnic groups integrated with the Han Chinese and adopted Chinese culture. However, when political and social instability broke out following the death of Emperor Wu, some tribes seized the opportunity to move further into China, displacing thousands of ethnic Chinese in the process.

Between around 304 and 439, the original Five Barbarian states further fragmented into sixteen smaller independent ones. The result was constant civil war and shifting of alliances. The ensuing chaos resulted in around one in eight ethnic Chinese migrating to Southern China.

Cultural Flowering

Between 420 and 589, the many independent states were broadly divided into the Northern Dynasties and the Southern Dynasties. Civil war continued throughout the period, as did the mass migration of people.

Despite the instability caused by the barbarian invasions and ongoing civil war, this was a time of creativity. In common with the new thinking of the 'Hundred Schools of Thought' that emerged in the 6th and 3rd Centuries BC, so technology, science, poetry and religious thought flourished amidst the chaos and upheaval of the 5th and 6th Centuries AD.

A major innovation during this time of warfare, was the invention of the stirrup. A very basic form of stirrup, in the form of a rope with a toe loop, had been used in India, possibly as early as 500 BC. However, the first evidence of a full two-sided stirrup, which must have been used by heavy cavalry at the time of the Jin Dynasty, was found in today's Nanjing in the form of a funerary figurine dating from 322 AD.

Advances were also made during the same period in the field of mathematics and astronomy. For example, Zu Chongzhi, a talented young mathematician undertaking research at the Imperial Nanjing University, produced a formula for the volume of the sphere and for the value of *pi*. Chongzhi is also credited with calculating the number of days in the year and the distance of Jupiter from Earth, the results of which are remarkably close to calculations of today.

Poetry, painting and calligraphy also flourished in both the Northern and Southern Dynasties, although there was a difference in style. In the South the work was light-hearted and flowery while in the North it was more mundane and basic.

This probably reflects the fact that the North was beset with war and suffering, while in the South there was a sense of hope and new beginnings as refugees from the North began a new life. The same trend was evident in philosophical thought. In the North, philosophers displayed despondency and some retreated from society becoming mountain hermits.

Religious Thought

For many, the ongoing instability raised questions about the meaning of life. In the midst of suffering, traditional Confucianism and Taoism failed to provide a satisfactory solution. It was in this context that Buddhism, with its comprehensive doctrine on suffering, became increasingly popular.

Buddhism first entered China with missionaries from India in the 1st Century AD. According to tradition, the first Buddhist temple, known as the White Horse Temple, was built by Emperor Ming of Han around 50 AD. The temple was named after the white horses that supposedly carried the Buddhist scriptures along the Silk Road from India to China. By the 2nd Century AD, a Buddhist monk from Parthia, had translated a large corpus of scripture into Chinese, some of which is extant.

Initially Buddhism was rejected by the Confucian and Taoist establishment on the grounds that the religion had nothing positive to contribute to society. By the 5th Century, however, Buddhism had become inculturated into Chinese society and was therefore more acceptable to the Chinese hierarchy.

This was partly due to the incorporation of some Taoist concepts into Buddhist teaching and also the fact that by the 5th Century, people had access to the scriptures in their own language. Gradually Buddhism in China moved away from its Indian roots and evolved into a distinctive form of Chinese Buddhism that would eventually spread to Korea, Japan and Vietnam.

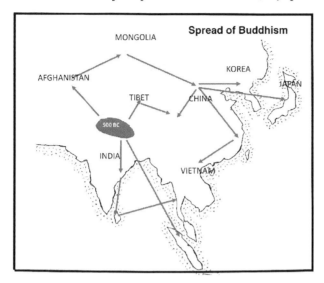

The Sui Dynasty: 581-618

The Sui Dynasty, which lasted less than forty years, was a pivotal period in Chinese history and in many ways laid the foundation for the following Tang Dynasty.

The Sui was founded in 581 by Yang Jian, an official of the Northern Zhou Dynasty. He took the imperial name of Emperor Wen of Sui. Being a Buddhist, he patronised Buddhist teaching and temple building, which contributed to the continuing spread of Buddhism.

Emperor Wen's greatest achievement was to unite the Northern Dynasties and Southern Dynasties into a reunited China. He then introduced many administrative reforms, one of the most important being the 'Equal Field System'.

Under this system, all land belonged to the Government. It was then parcelled out to individuals, including slaves and women. The amount of land allocated was dependent upon a person's ability to farm the land. For example, women received less than able-bodied men. The aim was to make the population self-sufficient and stop landlords acquiring too much land and therefore becoming too powerful. The system also generated extra income for the government through rent and taxation. When a tenant died, the land returned to the Government for redistribution. An exception was made for farmers growing mulberry trees. Being the source of the valuable silk worm industry, continuity of mulberry tree farming was considered essential.

During his reign, Emperor Wen commissioned vast building projects. Apart from strengthening the Great Wall, he is credited with construction of the thousand-mile long Grand Canal. The canal starts in Beijing in the North and connects with the inland city of Luoyang, which at the time was the Sui capital. It ends in Hangzhou near modern Shanghai. Apart from providing a link between the Yangtse and Yellow Rivers, numerous minor rivers fed into the Grand Canal, giving rural communities access to the waterways and therefore a means of transportation.

The main shipment at the time was grain, but it also enabled the transportation of Sui troops from one region of China to another. As with the Great Wall, the canal was built by conscript labour and resulted in a huge loss of life. Furthermore, as construction costs rose, the burden fell on the population through higher taxation.

Despite the human costs involved, the economy grew and China entered a time of prosperity. The Grand Canal continues to provide important trade links within China. It is now a UNESCO World Heritage Site and is a famous tourist destination.

These ambitious building projects contributed to the downfall of the Sui Dynasty. Under the second Emperor, Yang, riots broke out among the conscript workers and the people rebelled over high taxes. The situation was aggravated by a series of failed military campaigns against the Kingdom of Goguryeo in North Korea.

The Tang Dynasty: 618-907

We get most of our information about the Tang Dynasty from *The Old Book of Tang,* written around 907, and *The New Book of Tang* that was compiled during the Song Dynasty (960-1279). Both manuscripts form part of the official *Twenty-Four Histories* of China.

The Tang Dynasty was founded by Li Yuan, Duke of Tang, who claimed to be a direct descendent of Laozi, the founder of Taoism. Under the Sui Dynasty, he had served as Governor of the North Eastern province of today's Shanxi. In 617, encouraged by his sons, Li Yuan rose in rebellion against Emperor Yang of Sui. Li Yuan's daughter, Princess Pingyang, also took part in the rebellion. She personally led her own army, known as 'the Army of the Lady'.

Emperor Yang of Sui was murdered during the rebellion and his 13-year old son installed as puppet Emperor. Shortly after, the boy was forced to abdicate the throne to Li Yuan, who then became first Emperor of the Tang Dynasty, taking the name Gaozu.

Apart from an interregnum, between 690 and 705, when the Empress Dowager founded the short-lived Zhou Dynasty, the Tang ruled for almost 300 years. The Tang capital city of Chang'an, today's Xian, had around 80 million inhabitants and was probably the most populous in the world at that time.

The Tang inherited many administrative reforms that had been put in place by the Sui, for example the Equal Field System mentioned above. Emperor Gaozu also kept in place the Sui Government structure known as the Three Departments and Six Ministries. The Three Departments included the Secretariat, the Chancellery and the Department of State, all three being responsible for drafting and implementing Government policy.

The Ministries were responsible for Personnel, Rites, War, Justice, Works and Revenue. While the Departments were abolished under the Ming Dynasty (1368-1644), the Ministries continued until the end of the Qing Dynasty in 1912.

Such a complex system required an efficient Civil Service. The Tang established a selection process for admission that would remain in place until the end of the Qing Dynasty. Selection was only open to male Confucian scholars who had to pass demanding examinations before being accepted. Apart from Confucian classics, the examinations included poetry, rhetoric, deportment, speech and calligraphy. Those who passed the selection process became known as Mandarins.

Zhou Dynasty: 690 – 705

The fifteen years' interregnum, known as the Zhou Dynasty, (not to be confused with the first Zhou Dynasty of the 2nd Century BC) was important in two ways. First, it was the only time in Chinese history when a woman ruled as 'Emperor' in her own right. Second, it marked a time of expansion deep into Central Asia that was to affect the ethnic and religious makeup of China for many centuries.

The founder of the Dynasty, Wu Zetian, was born around 624 into the family of a wealthy timber merchant. She was well educated and it is said that Li Yuan, the future Emperor Gaozu, became friendly with her father and frequently visited the family home.

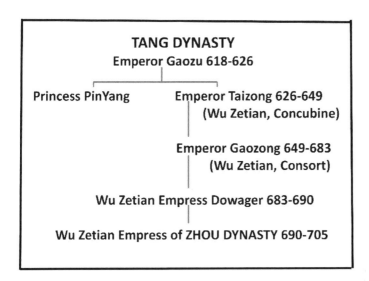

TANG DYNASTY
Emperor Gaozu 618-626

Princess PinYang   Emperor Taizong 626-649
                   (Wu Zetian, Concubine)

                  Emperor Gaozong 649-683
                   (Wu Zetian, Consort)

Wu Zetian Empress Dowager 683-690

Wu Zetian Empress of ZHOU DYNASTY 690-705

When Wu Zetian was 14, she became Imperial Concubine to Li Yuan's son, the Emperor Taizong. It is said that she did not particularly like Taizong, who was almost thirty years her senior but she probably compensated for this by continuing but she with her studies, particularly in history and politics.

Emperor Taizong died in 649 and Wu Zetian was forced to enter a Buddhist monastery because she had not produced a child. However, her time as a nun was short lived. The succeeding Emperor, Gaozong, took her as one of his senior concubines.

Gaozong was only 21 when he became Emperor. Because he was inexperienced and sickly, he soon came under the influence of the able, and ambitious, Wu Zetian. In 655, she became Empress consort and by the time of Gaozong's death, in 683, she had been ruler of the Empire in all but name.

In 690, after a period as Dowager Empress, she declared herself Empress of a new Dynasty. She named it the Zhou because she believed she was a descendent of the first Zhou Dynasty. She also became a Buddhist because according to strict Confucianism, a woman could not rule as Emperor.

In February 705, at the age of eighty, Wu Zetian abdicated the throne in favour of her son Li Xian. The second Zhou Dynasty came to an end and Li Xian became Emperor Zhongzong of a restored Tang Dynasty.

Wu Zetian has gone down in history as a cruel and despotic ruler who murdered her close relatives in order to gain and to hold on to power. While there may well be some truth in these accusations, she proved to be an able ruler. As a child she had studied history and politics. From the age of fourteen she was close to the seat of Imperial power and her years as Empress Consort and Empress Dowager left her well equipped to rule in her own right.

One of Wu Zetian's greatest skills was her ability to discern a person's suitability for a senior position. Consequently, she surrounded herself with the most able and trusted officials. She also placed meritocracy above aristocracy and opened up the Civil Service examination system to commoners.

Foreign Relations

The various Central Asian kingdoms that were conquered by the Tang, received protectorate status in exchange for tribute. Each State was ruled by a military governor, known as a *Jeidushi,* who had his own army and in some cases the authority to collect taxes.

However, since the rise of Islam in the 7th Century, the region had become politically unstable. When the Islamic Caliphate of the Umayyads conquered the Persian Sassanid Empire in 651, Prince Peroz III, son of Yazdegerd, the last Sassanid King, fled to China. The Sassanids had always enjoyed good relations with the Chinese, largely on account of their mutual trade interests along the Silk Road.

Prince Peroz was welcomed by the Imperial Court. He later became a General in the Tang Army and the men in his entourage were given senior positions. Many Persian refugees would later find refuge in China.

In 750, another Muslim Caliphate, the Abbasids, overthrew the Umayyads. The Abbasids then embarked upon an aggressive campaign to conquer Central Asia and particularly the cities along the Silk Road. They were joined by traders and merchants along the trade route who probably allied with the Abbasids against the Umayyads for pragmatic reasons.

The Abbasids allied with the Tibetan Empire, at that time an enemy of the Tang. In May 751, a major battle took place at Talas, on the border between present day Kazakhstan and Kyrgyzstan. The Abbasid and Tibetan Armies defeated the Imperial troops of the Tang. This was partly because many of the Karluks, a nomadic Turkic confederation, who were fighting as mercenaries with the Tang, defected to the Abbasids.

The Battle of Talas marked the end of Chinese expansion in the West for another 400 years. It also marked the beginning of Islamicisation throughout Central Asia. The dominance of Islam in the region further affected Buddhists. Travel along the Silk Road between India and China became more difficult for Buddhists and added to the already distancing of Chinese Buddhism from its Indian roots.

Many Chinese soldiers were taken as prisoners by the Abbasids following the Battle of Talas. It is traditionally believed that these prisoners then passed their knowledge of papermaking and block printing to the Abbasids. Through the Abbasid capital of Baghdad, these skills then travelled to the West via Islamic Spain.

An Lushan Rebellion: 755 – 763

An Lushan was a General (*Jiedushi*) in the Tang army during the reign of Emperor Xuanzong. As a favourite of the Emperor, he was awarded the Governorship of three Northern garrisons: the

Pinglu, Fanyang and Hedong, as well as a luxurious home in the capital city of Chang'an.

However, he was ambitious for greater power and he took advantage of the Empire's weakness in the aftermath of its defeat at the Battle of Talas. He was also able to incite the impoverished population in the North to rebel against the growing excesses of the Tang Court.

In December 755, An Lushan led an army of some 200,000 men from Fanyang, near today's Beijing, down the Grand Canal towards Luoyang. Along the way, many Tang officials joined him and within a year he had arrived at Luoyang, where he declared himself Emperor of a rival Yan Dynasty. By the end of 756, An Lushan had succeeded in taking the capital city of Chang'an. Despite military support from the Abbasids, the Emperor was forced to admit defeat and flee to Sichuan in the South.

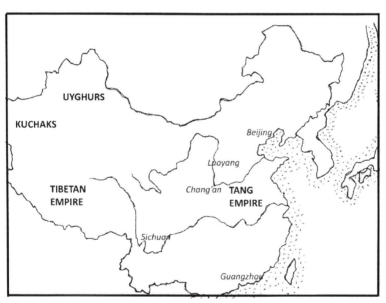

The An Lushan rebellion continued for another eight years. The overall death toll was devasting. From an estimated 9 million households recorded in the 755 census, the number dropped to

3 million households by 764. Two-thirds of the population had died, either from the fighting or due to widespread starvation.

The rebellion marked a turning point for the Tang Dynasty. The Western protectorates in Central Asia were never regained because Imperial troops were recalled to protect the capital of Chang'an. At the same time, Imperial authority declined as regional warlords seized power.

This political instability was matched by a decline in the economy The Tang Emperor had borrowed money from the Uyghurs to help put down the rebellion and the resulting debt further exacerbated an already failing economy.

Events surrounding the upheaval also contributed to a change in the ethnic mix of China. Persian refugees from the former Sassanid Empire and Arabs from the Umayyad Empire continued to find refuge in China. Lastly, many Abbasid Arabs who were originally enemies of the Tang, became allies and started to settle in the major cities.

Guangzhou Massacre 878-879

Large numbers of Persians and Arabs settled in Yangzhou, on the Grand Canal and Guangzhou on the coast of the South China Sea. By the 9th Century, Guangzhou had become a wealthy seaport with trade links as far as the Indian Ocean and the Persian Gulf. Due to the political instability in Central Asia, the sea route between Persia and China was preferable to the overland Silk Road.

Tang period coins, discovered in the Straits of Hormuz, provides further evidence of maritime contact between Chinese and Persians. *The Old Book of Tang* also makes reference to a Chinese soldier, who had been taken prisoner by the Abbasids, travelling home by sea after many years in captivity.

In 760, during the chaos of the An Lushan rebellion, Persian and Arab merchants living in Yangzhou were massacred by disaffected rebels. Exact statistics are unknown, but the victims were targets of xenophobes resentful of the merchants' wealth.

We have better evidence, from *The Old Book of Tang,* of the Guangzhou Massacre that was carried out in 878. This massacre was led by Huang Chao, a salt smuggler and rebel. His anti-Tang feelings were strengthened by his anger at having failed the Government entrance examinations which he had entered several times.

Huang Chao rampaged across the country, gathering support from disaffected farmers who had been suffering the effects of flooding and high taxation. When he reached Guangzhou, his men not only killed Persians and Arabs, but also Jews, Zoroastrians and Nestorian Christians. In 451 the Council of Chalcedon had declared the Nestorians to be heretical and from that time they had gradually migrated Eastwards, some finally reaching China.

The final death toll resulting from the massacre of foreigners in Guangzhou in 878, is estimated as being between 120,000 and 200,000.

The An Lushan rebellion marked the beginning of a slow decline for the Tang Dynasty. Its demise followed a familiar pattern that was repeated throughout Imperial Chinese history. As Imperial power waned, feudal warlords became increasingly independent with their own armies and ability to raise taxes. Succession crises often ran in parallel with civil war and finally the Empire disintegrated into separate Kingdoms until the rise of a new leader capable of reuniting the country. The Tang Dynasty collapsed in 907 and China would not be reunited until 960 with the rise of the Song Dynasty.

Conclusion

Apart from the short interregnum under the Zhou, the Tang Dynasty ruled for almost three hundred years. It was a pivotal time in Chinese history and its success in the early years was partly due to the innovations inherited from the Sui Dynasty. For example, The Equal Field System and the governmental Three Departments and Six Ministries were to prove long-lasting, some remaining in place through to the end of the Qing Dynasty in 1912.

It is interesting to note that one of the causes for the collapse of the Sui in 618 was due to its failed attempt to conquer Goguryeo, today's North Korea. Despite the Sui's superiority in numbers, the Koreans repeatedly pushed the Chinese back. Throughout history North Korea has fought to maintain its independence, no more so than today.

The fifteen years between 690 and 705 under Empress Wu Zetian were remarkable in several ways, not least because she was the only woman in Chinese history to rule in her own right. Wu Zetian, like so many powerful women throughout history, has been portrayed as a cruel and manipulating despot. There seems to be a tendency among some historians to credit the success of many such women to pure despotism rather than acknowledge their skills and ability to rule. Alternatively, they are portrayed as being influenced by a circle of close court officials, or even lovers, as was the case with Catherine the Great.

In the case of Wu Zetian, she was probably no more, or no less, despotic than other rulers of the time. However, the fact that she became influential at court in her teens and survived into her eighties, when she abdicated the throne, is evidence of her ability.

It was during Wu Zetian's reign that the Chinese made great inroads into Central Asia, establishing vassal states among the various Turkic tribes. The fact that the region was later lost to the Chinese was due to events taking place thousands of miles away, in the West.

The rise of Islam in the early 7th Century was to have a ripple affect across Europe, Africa and Asia. China first felt the consequences when Persian refugees, including members of the

Sassanid royal family, fled to the Tang court. From this point on, waves of Persian refugees, fleeing the Muslim Umayyads, would travel to China and Persian music and poetry would become a feature of Tang court life. Another wave of refugees, this time Arabs, would follow the same route when the Umayyad Caliphate was overthrown by the Abbasid Caliphate in 750.

Due to the political instability in Central Asia, travel along the Silk Road became difficult, at times even impossible. Consequently, merchants took the sea route from Persia via the Indian Ocean to the South China Sea, Japan and the Korean Peninsula. This led to the rise of wealthy maritime cities such as Guangzhou.

By the middle of the 8th Century, the ethnic mix of China had changed considerably. The Northern part of the country was populated by large numbers of Mongol nomadic tribal people who had crossed the border and become integrated with the Chinese. Persian and Arab refugees had become wealthy merchants and had settled in the large cities, along with smaller communities of Jews, Zoroastrians and Christians. Abbasid, Turkic and Uyghur mercenaries fought alongside the Chinese in the Imperial Army.

When the An Lushan rebellion broke out in 755, causing social and political upheaval, foreigners living in Yangzhou and Guangzhou became scapegoats and thousands were massacred. This would not be the last time in Chinese history that foreigners would be targeted in this way.

The An Lushan rebellion marked the beginning of the decline of the Tang Dynasty. In 907, Emperor Ai, the last of the Tang emperors was deposed and once more the country fragmented, this time into the 'Five Dynasties and Ten Kingdoms' period that was to last for the next fifty years.

*****

CHAPTER FOUR

The Mongols: 1271-1368

The Song Dynasty: 960-1279

During the Five Dynasties and Ten Kingdoms period, which lasted from 907 to 960, China was once more divided into a Northern and Southern region. Five consecutive dynasties ruled in the North, while in the South ten small independent kingdoms existed, very often, in parallel with each other.

The last dynasty to rule in the North was known as the Later Zhou. In 960, a military general named Zhao Kuangyin launched a coup against the Emperor of Later Zhou. He then went on to found the Song Dynasty, taking the name Emperor Taizu of Song.

The Song Dynasty, in common with other Chinese Dynasties, was divided into two periods: The Northern Song (960-1127) and the Southern Song (1127-1279).

The Northern Song: 960-1127

Emperor Taizu established his capital at Kaifeng, which soon became one of the largest cities in the world. In order to reduce the power of the military, which posed a threat to his rule, he appointed administrators rather than generals as regional governors.

At the same time, Taizu improved the civil service examination system in order to ensure that only the best qualified candidates entered the civil service. He also commissioned a team of cartographers to produce detailed maps of the provinces, which was essential for efficient government. Other innovations included the introduction of paper banknotes and the development of the first water-driven astronomical clock.

Coming from a military background, Emperor Taizu wanted to ensure that he had the best military hardware that was available.

He promoted the use of gunpowder and he established arsenals in Kaifeng, manufacturing grenades and cannon as well as traditional firearms.

During the period of the Northern Song, diplomatic relations flourished with Egypt, the Byzantine Empire, the Chola Empire of India, Central Asia and the Goryeon Kingdom (today's Korea). Tensions continued, however, with neighbours nearer to home, namely the Khitans in the Northeast and Tanguts, also known as the Western Xia, in the Northwest.

During the reign of Emperor Shenzong of Song (1067-1085), internal conflict broke out over the issue of Government reforms. When the economist and statesman, Wang Anshi, proposed a series of socioeconomic measures, known as the 'New Policies', he was opposed by the conservative Chancellor Sima Guang. The ongoing tensions weakened the central government, making the nation vulnerable to outside attack.

The Great Jin: 1115 - 1234

While the central government of the Song Dynasty was beginning to show signs of weakness, the Jurchens, a Manchurian tribal confederation in the North, were on the rise. At that time, the Jurchens were vassals of the Liao (Khitan) Dynasty. However, in 1112, Aguda, a leader of the Wanyan, a tribe within the Jurchen confederation, succeeded in uniting all other Jurchen tribes in opposition to their Khitan overlords.

Having established his position, in 1115 Aguda was proclaimed Emperor Taizu of the Jin Dynasty, also known as the Jurchen Dynasty and sometimes referred to as the Great Jin, to differentiate it from the earlier Jin (265-420).

The Song and the Great Jin had a common enemy in the Northern Liao. Consequently, they formed an alliance, known as the Alliance at Sea, so named because the envoys crossed the Yellow Sea, the waters separating China from the Korean Peninsula, in order to conduct their negotiations.

The alliance lasted from 1115 until 1123, during which time the Song continued to decline. Soon after Emperor Taizu of Jin died, his younger brother, who became Emperor Taizong, broke the alliance and went to war against the Song. Many anti-Song nobles joined the Jurchens and for the next ninety years the Song and Jin were in a state of intermittent war.

Although the Jin had a weak navy, they had a stronger army than the Song, largely due to the many defections of disaffected Song to their ranks. In 1127, the Jin seized the capital of Kaifeng and imprisoned the Song Emperor, together with his family. One son, however, managed to escape to the South where he founded the Southern Song.

With the collapse of the Northern Song, some three million Manchu Jurchens migrated into Northern China. Many were given prime land and prominent military and government positions. Initially a minority Jurchen people governed a majority Han population. In time, however, the Jurchens became sinicised, partly through inter-marriage. Consequently, the Jin inherited not only Song culture, but also its many scientific innovations.

The new Jin Dynasty faced two major problems. In the short term, the government had to find ways of integrating the many different ethnic groups that now came under its rule.

In the longer term, they faced an increasing threat from the Mongols of the Northwest. In 1123, the Jin began a major reinforcement of the Great Wall. Over a period of seventy years, they built border fortresses and an elaborate system of ditches stretching some 2,000 kilometres. The Jin walls, which can still be seen today, became known as Mingchang Old Great Wall and the Mingchang New Great Wall.

Genghis Khan

For many decades, the Mongol tribes had been conducting raids into Chinese territory. They seized livestock and captured men for their armies and women and children as slaves. The Chinese responded with punitive action. On one occasion the Jin crucified Ambaghai, Khan of the Khamag clan. It was an act that would not be forgotten by the Mongols.

Most Mongol tribes were vassals of the Chinese and the Jin had always applied a policy of divide and rule. In this way Mongol power was kept in check and reduced the threat of large-scale invasion.

However, everything changed in 1206 when Temujin of the Borjigin clan, managed to subdue all the other Mongol clans and tribes and bring them under his sole rule. In recognition, he was proclaimed the Great Khan, (Khagan), better known in the West as Genghis Khan.

When Wanyan Yongji ascended the Jin throne in 1210, he sent a delegation to Genghis Khan demanding the Mongol leader's submission. According to tradition, the Great Khan spat on the ground, turned his back in contempt and rode off. He then called a *kuraltai*, or great assembly of the elders, to discuss the best way to deal with the Jin.

Following the *kuraltai*, he spent three days praying to the great god *Tengri* and reflecting on the treatment of his tribes by the Jin. He especially wanted revenge for the crucifixion of Ambaghai Khan.

In 1211, Genghis prepared his attack on the Jin. He had already secured an alliance with the Khitans in the North and also the Western Xia. But his greatest asset was to be his general, Subatai.

Subatai was born in 1175 to the Uriankhai clan, a forest-dwelling people from Siberia. He and Temujin (Genghis Khan) had known each other from childhood, during the difficult, years of Temujin's life. Coming from the forest, rather than the plains, Subatai differed from most Mongol warriors in that he was not a natural horseman. Despite this, he is recognised as one of the world's greatest military commanders.

When he was still in his teens, Subatai was permitted to attend war councils and listen in to discussions on strategy. By the age of 22, he was given his own command. By the time of his death in 1248, at the age of 72, he had conquered over thirty-two nations and led successful military campaigns into Hungary, Poland and Russia.

Collapse of the Jin

By 1211, many Khitan and Jurchen rebels had joined the Great Khan. He was also aided by members of the Ongud tribe that lived near the Great Wall. Although ethnically Mongolian, the Onguds were Christian, belonging to the Nestorian Church.

The Onguds had traditionally acted as border guards for the Jin, but Genghis secured their allegiance by marrying his daughter to a son of the Ongud Chief. Having reneged against the Jin, the Onguds then used their knowledge of the area to guide the Mongol army of around 50,000 men, into Jin territory.

Between August and October 1211, a prolonged battle, known as the Battle of Yehuling, took place in Hebei Province between the Mongol forces and the Jin. It was to be a decisive victory for the Mongols.

Following the battle, the Jin Emperor Wanyan Yongji was assassinated by one of his generals and was succeeded by Emperor Xuanzong.

The Mongols then went on to besiege Zhongdu, present day Beijing. At the time they were expert in the field of siege warfare and the city was trapped for four years, reducing the people to cannibalism in order to survive. In 1214, the Mongols offered to lift the siege under the terms of a humiliating treaty. Emperor Xuanzong agreed to the terms, thereby saving Zhongdu. He then moved the capital city to Kaifeng.

The Southern Song, who were also enemies of the Jin, allied with the Mongols. Against all odds, the Jin managed to survive constant attack from the Mongols for another thirty years.

Finally, in 1233, Kaifeng fell and Aizong, the last Emperor of the Jin fled. The following year he committed suicide, marking the end of the Jin Dynasty.

Kublai Khan

When Genghis Khan died in 1227, he divided his Empire between his four sons; Jochi, the eldest was given the Caucasus and Russia. The second son, Chagatai, received Central Asia. The youngest son, Tolui, was given the smallest region which was Mongolia, the homeland of Mongols.

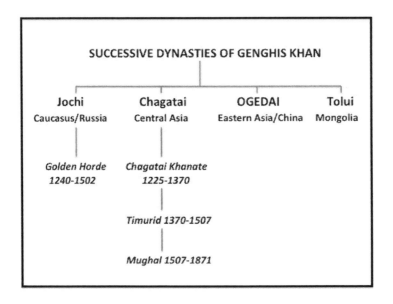

SUCCESSIVE DYNASTIES OF GENGHIS KHAN

Jochi	Chagatai	OGEDAI	Tolui
Caucasus/Russia	Central Asia	Eastern Asia/China	Mongolia
Golden Horde	*Chagatai Khanate*		
1240-1502	*1225-1370*		
	Timurid 1370-1507		
	Mughal 1507-1871		

The third son, Ogedai, whom Genghis considered the most able, was made Great Khan and received Eastern Asia and China. It was under Ogedai, who ruled from 1229 to 1241, that the Jin fell to the Mongols. At the death of Ogedai, his son Guyuk, who succeeded him as Khan, continued the battle to subdue the Southern Song.

Whereas Ogedai had been appointed by Genghis Khan, subsequent Khagans were elected at the *kuraltai* in the Mongol capital of Karakorum. All Khans from across the Empire were expected to attend the election, from as far away as Sarai in Russia. Given the distances involved, it could be many months, or even years, before the process was complete. In the interim, it was normal for the wife of the deceased Khagan to act as Regent.

Kublai Khan was the fourth son of Tolui and he was a grandson of Genghis Khan. As a child, he and his brothers were with the Great Khan during the campaign against the Khwarazmian Empire, an event that brought the whole of Central Asia, as far as the Black Sea and Persian Gulf, into the Mongol orbit of power.

When Ogedei's troops beat the Jin at the Battle of Yehuling in 1211, Kublai was awarded the Province of Hebei and he later became Viceroy over North China. During this time, he brought the Kingdom of Dali, (modern Hunan), under Mongol control as a vassal state, permitting the royal family to remain as nominal rulers, but with the Mongol as overlords.

In 1260, Goryeo, on the Korean peninsula became a vassal state and the same year Kublai was elected to succeed his older brother, Mongke, as Great Khan. However, the election was challenged by the youngest brother, Ariq Boke.

Consequently, civil war broke out signalling the end of a unified Mongol Empire. Thereafter, Kublai Khan's title as Great Khan over the whole Empire was purely symbolic. The great Mongol Empire was divided. The Golden Horde that ruled Russia, and the Ilkhanate in Central Asia, became virtually independent.

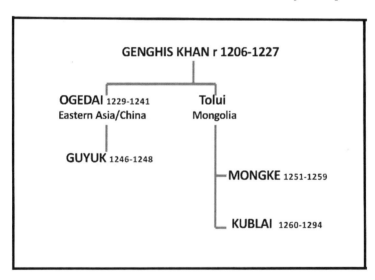

The Yuan Dynasty

It was to be Kublai Khan, the fifth Khagan of the Mongol Empire, who would finally defeat the Southern Song at the Battle of Yamen. Rather than face dishonour, the eight-year old Song Emperor, together with his entire family, committed suicide. The year was 1279. It marked the beginning of the Yuan Dynasty, the first non-Han Chinese dynasty to rule over the whole of China.

From an early age, Kublai showed a great interest in both Buddhism and Chinese culture. The appeal of Buddhism stemmed from the fact that his wet-nurse had been Buddhist and he remained very close to her for many years. He studied Buddhism under the best monk scholars of the time and he appointed Buddhists as his personal advisers.

Whenever conflict broke out between Buddhists and Daoists, as frequently happened, Kublai ruled in favour of the Buddhists, on one occasion ordering that the Buddhist monks seize all the Daoist temples.

Kublai placed great emphasis on meritocracy. From his time with Genghis Khan in Central Asia, he had come into contact with some of the most skilled engineers, scientists and administrators of the Islamic world and he appointed the most able Muslims to positions of importance. He also included Kipchaks and Alans from the Eurasian Steppes, as well as Russians, into his elite Imperial Guard.

Early in his reign, Kublai Khan established twelve administrative districts, eight of which he put under Muslim administrators. He appointed cartographers to map the entire length of the Silk Road, which was now under control of the various Mongol powers.

The Yuan Dynasty built upon the military innovations of the Jin, such as gunpowder and hand grenades. They were less successful in naval warfare, however. This was proven in their abortive attempts to invade Japan in 1274 and 1281. In part this was due to bad weather, but also the Mongol ships were inferior to those of the Japanese.

Attempts to subdue Burma and Java were also unsuccessful; this time due to the inhospitable tropical climate which did not suit troops from the nomadic steppe. The failure to take Japan, Burma and Java was significant because it broke the myth of Mongol invincibility.

Pax Mongolica

The period of Mongol rule during the 13th and 14th Centuries is often referred to as the *Pax Mongolica.* In common with the earlier *Pax Romana*, it was a time of relative peace and stability that allowed communication and trade to flourish.

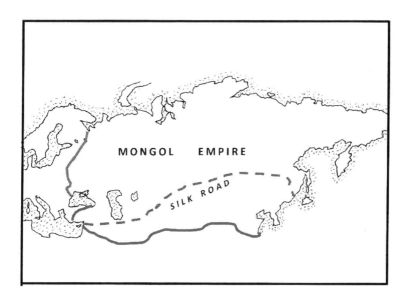

For the first time in history, the entire length of the Silk Road was unified under one power, linking East with West. Previously travellers had to pass through different states, each with its own currency and road tax. The journey was dangerous, with a constant threat of attack from bandits. Under the Mongols, a common currency was introduced, as well as standardised weights and measures. The use of paper money avoided the need to carry large amounts of coin.

The Silk Road also provided an efficient postal service. Known as the *Yam,* messengers would only travel a distance of some 15 to 20 miles to the next relay station. Here they would be provided with board and lodging and the message was transferred to another rider with a fresh horse for the next part of the journey.

Travellers were protected along the journey by Mongol troops who carried out their duties according to the *Yasa,* or Mongol law. For example, robbery and even the stealing of livestock, which had previously been common practice, became a punishable offence and in order to protect personal property, a 'lost and found' system operated.

Cities located along the route became very wealthy. As well as being centres of trade, they were meeting places where travellers from many nations, cultures and ethnicities could exchange knowledge and share ideas from across the known world.

Apart from the overland Silk Road, the Mongols also established a Maritime Silk Road carrying goods by sea from the China coast to the Indian Ocean, Arabian Gulf and Red Sea.

As a result of improved communication and safer travel, the *Pax Mongolica* witnessed an upsurge in Europeans travelling to China. This was especially so under Kublai Khan during the Yuan Dynasty.

Marco Polo

The best-known European traveller at that time was the Venetian merchant Marco Polo. His father, Niccolo Polo and uncle, Maffeo Polo, had already visited the court of Kublai Khan. In 1271, they set off for a second time to China, but this time they took the 17-year old Marco with them.

The adventurers spent 24 years travelling across Central and Eastern Asia, spending considerable time in China and Mongolia. When they returned home, Venice was at war with Genoa. Marco got caught up in the fighting and was captured. He spent several months in prison and it was during this time that he dictated the story of his epic journey to a fellow inmate. The result was the well-known book, *The Travels of Marco Polo.*

There has been much debate about the authenticity of Marco's account, since there was no single authoritative version. Rather, various individual manuscripts were gathered together, the content of which was often contradictory.

It has even been suggested that Marco did not get as far as China at all since there are apparent gaps in his account. For example, there is no mention of the Great Wall, tea, or foot-binding. Those who defend his account claim that other travellers of the time make no mention of these things either. They point out that the Mongol Dynasty of the Yuan had a very negative view of the Wall. After all, it had been built over the previous centuries in order to keep them out. Marco's supporters also claim that foot-binding, that became a common practice under the Song in the 10th Century, was not a Mongol tradition. Furthermore, even if practiced by the Han Chinese, it was rare and only then, in a mild form.

Ibn Battuta

Another famous traveller to visit China during the Yuan period was Ibn Battuta, the Moroccan explorer. In 1332, he embarked upon an extensive journey that took him across Central and South-East Asia, arriving in China in 1345.

Ibn Battuta arrived in Guanzhou, on the South-eastern Coast if China and spent most of his time with Muslim communities. In his own account of his travels, he describes how Muslims had their own mosques and hospitals and lived in a separate quarter to the Chinese. He says how impressed he is with the beautiful silks, porcelain and paper money that is so much easier to carry than coins.

Unlike Marco Polo, Ibn Battuta does refer to what was probably the Great Wall. He tells that people spoke about the 'ramparts of

Yajuj and Majuj' that were about sixty days' travel from Guanzhou. He did not meet anyone who had seen the 'ramparts', but it seems that the Muslims thought that the wall had been built to keep out Gog and Magog, who are referred to in the Quran.

Christian Missionaries

Whatever the truth may be regarding Marco Polo and his travels, his book, *The Travels of Marco Polo,* probably more than anything else, created a fascination in the West for the Orient, and especially China.

But he was not the only European to travel to China at that time. Under Kublai Khan, a period of religious tolerance reigned. Muslims, Jews and Nestorian Christians had been living in China for generations. However, the opening up of the Silk Road enabled Western missionaries to travel Eastwards with a mission to convert the 'heathen' to the Christian Faith.

The first missionary of any importance was John of Montecorvino, an Italian Franciscan priest. He had already made a name for himself in 1272, as one of the prime negotiators working to reunite the Eastern Orthodox and Western Catholic Churches. The early Church had officially split in 1054 over political and theological issues. In 1204, during the Fourth Crusade, relations deteriorated even further following the sack of Constantinople, the seat of the Orthodox Church, by Western Crusaders.

John of Montecorvino was also instrumental in attempting to form an alliance between Western Christians and the Mongols (Franco-Mongol Alliance). The purpose was to defeat their common enemy, the Seljuk and Mamluk Islamic forces, but the alliance was never sealed.

During this same period, there was much talk of the legendary Prester (Presbyter) John. His name was often associated with the St. Thomas Church in India. Some thought he was a Persian

King. Others claimed he was Patriarch of the Eastern Nestorian Church. During the Crusader period, many Christians believed that Prester John would come from the East to save the Holy City of Jerusalem from the 'infidel'.

In 1275, John of Montecorvino travelled along the Silk Road to Persia. While there he met the Nestorian Rabban Bar Sauma, who acted as Kublai Khan's Ambassador to the West. As a result of this meeting, Kublai Khan asked the Pope that John be permitted to travel to China, first to explain to the Khan the basics of Christian doctrine and then to teach the people the Christian Faith.

Eventually John set off for China. He reached India in 1291 where he spent some time preaching and baptising the people. When he arrived at Khanbaliq, the Mongol term for Beijing, in 1294, Kublai Khan had died. Despite not having the same enthusiasm for Christianity, his successor, Temur Khan, welcomed the missionary and permitted him to begin his work.

Not surprisingly, the Eastern Nestorian Church resented the arrival of the Western missionaries. Despite their opposition, in 1299, John was able to build the first Catholic Church in China. According to tradition, he bought around 150 boys between the ages of 7 and 11 from their parents. He then taught the boys the Christian Faith and instructed them on how to assist at the Mass.

Apart from his normal missionary work, Montecorvino also translated the New Testament and the Psalms into the Uyghur language, the language used by the Mongol elite.

Due to the success of the mission to China, the Vatican sent seven Franciscan bishops to join John, the intention being to consecrate him as Archbishop of Khanbaliq (Beijing).

In 1338, ten years after the death of John Montecorvino, a further 50 priests were sent to China. However, in 1369, all Christians, of all denominations, were expelled from China. The days of religious tolerance had ended with the fall of the Yuan and the rise of the Ming.

Conclusion

The Song Dynasty, that lasted over three hundred years, from 960 to 1279, was a period that witnessed growth and prosperity as well as cultural and scientific innovation. In common with other periods of Chinese history, however, Song rule was divided into two distinct periods caused by invasions from the North.

From the beginning, the Song faced a threat from Jurchen tribes in the North as well as Tangut tribes in the West. And lurking in the background was the constant fear of the nomadic Mongols.

The Jurchens finally invaded in 1115 and founded the Great Jin Dynasty, which ruled over the Northern part of China. The Song fled to the South and founded the Southern Song Dynasty which survived until 1279.

The Jurchen invasions caused a mass migration of people from North to South. First, many Jurchens who had previously been vassals of the Liao, migrated across the border into China. This in turn led to Han Chinese Song people migrating to the South.

In order to minimise the power of the military, Jin territory was divided into provinces that were ruled by administrators rather than military governors. To improve efficiency, the Emperor commissioned cartographers to map out all provinces. Genghis Khan would later do the same along the route of the Silk Road.

Faced with the threat of the Mongols, the Jin reinforced the Great Walls by building extra fortifications and wide ditches. This was not sufficient to keep out the Mongols, however, and in 1211 the Great Khan, with the help of the Ongud tribes, crossed over into China.

Although the Jin Dynasty collapsed in 1234, the Southern Song managed to hold the Mongols off until 1279. In the meantime, Kublai Khan, a grandson of Genghis Khan, had been elected

Khagan and when the Song finally collapsed he founded the Yuan Dynasty, the first non-Han Chinese power to rule a united China.

The period of Yuan rule, that lasted from 1271 to 1368, is known as the *Pax Mongolica* because it is recognised as being a period of relative peace and stability. For the first time in history, the Silk Road came under one power and this enabled Kublai Khan to impose uniform taxes and regulations along the whole route. The presence of Mongol troops further ensured the safety of travellers.

With improved facilities and safer travel, cities developed and trade flourished, creating newfound wealth right across Central Asia. Explorers and missionaries followed in the wake of the traders.

The Yuan rule of the Mongols was open looking and religiously tolerant. Kublai Khan took a personal interest in Buddhism. He promoted numerous Muslims to senior positions. And he invited Christians missionaries to teach about Christianity.

All this would change in 1368 with the arrival of the Ming.

*****

CHAPTER FIVE

The Ming 1368-1644

A combination of events led to the fall of the Yuan Dynasty, starting with the disastrous flooding of the Yellow River. Throughout history the river had been prone to flooding, but in 1344, due to neglect of the irrigation system, it was particularly bad.

In an attempt to hold back the waters, the Emperor forced hundreds of thousands of peasants to build dams. The people were already suffering from heavy taxation in order to pay for the Yuan's expansionist wars. The appalling conditions they then faced building the dams, simply added to their discontent. To compound the people's misery, an outbreak of bubonic plague caused death and disease to spread throughout the population.

The White Lotus Society

As Yuan power declined, Mongol persecution of the majority Han population became commonplace, leading to resentment and thoughts of rebellion. It was in this context that the White Lotus Society emerged. Initially, a few members of the society joined other protest groups, but eventually they united to form a sizeable organisation known as the White Lotus Society.

The Society had both a religious and political agenda, both of which appealed to the discontented Han. It adopted a syncretistic, religion that was a mix of Buddhism and Manichaeism, which was a major religious movement founded by *Mani* in third century Persia. The group also held a strong belief in Maitreya, a future Buddha, or saviour figure, who would return at the 'End Times'. It was a millenarian belief that thrives on social instability and has manifested itself at various times within most religious traditions.

The Yuan Emperor banned the White Lotus Society in the 14th Century and consequently it went underground. However, it has re-emerged from time to time, especially during the 18th and 19th

Centuries. Today's Triad groups are thought to be loosely linked to the Organisation.

The Red Turban Rebellion 1351

The political aim of the White Lotus Society was to overthrow the Mongol led Yuan Dynasty and restore China to the Han people.

In 1351, Guo Zixing, a member of the Society, formed a small army known as the 'Red Turbans', named after their red banners and the red scarves they wrapped around their heads. The rebels' initial attempts to overthrow the Yuan failed and the leaders were executed.

The group survived however and for several years various factions fought among themselves for supremacy. In 1363, a major battle took place on Lake Poyang, which is China's largest fresh water lake and located in today's Jiangxi Province in the southeast. Said to be one of the largest naval battles in history, Zhu Yuanzhang, who was the son-in-law of Guo Zixing, used fire ships to defeat the tower ships, or 'floating fortresses' of his opponents.

Following this victory, Zhu Yuanzhang became leader of the Red Turban Army. He spent the following five years fighting the Yuan forces until they were eventually forced to surrender Khanbaliq (the Mongol name for modern Beijing) and retreat northwards towards Mongolia.

In 1368, Zhu Yuanzhang mounted the Temple of Heaven and claimed for himself the Mandate of Heaven, becoming known as Hongwu Emperor of the Ming Dynasty. Today the Temple and surrounding parkland is open to the public and it is a popular place for residents of Beijing to go for their morning exercise, ranging from tai chi, aerobics and dance.

Hongwu Emperor 1368-1398

The Hongwu Emperor (Zhu Yuanzhang) was born in 1328 into a poor peasant family. With insufficient food to feed all the children, his parents gave his older brothers away. When Zhu Yuanzhang was just 16, his entire family died from starvation and he entered a monastery. But the monastery offered no protection from the famine and when it ran out of food he was forced to leave.

After several years wandering as a beggar, Zhu Yuanzhang returned to the monastery where he learned to read and write. When he was 24, the monastery was destroyed by Yuan forces and it was at this time that Zhu Yuanzhang decided to join the rebel forces of the White Lotus Society in their fight against the Yuan.

Hongwu's suffering in his early life was to influence his policies during the early part of his reign. He dismissed all Mongol government officers and replaced them with Han Chinese officials. He also imposed a ban on Mongol dress and Mongol names. This led to a degree of persecution against the Mongols but it was not prolonged or on a large-scale.

Hongwu was a pragmatic, if authoritarian, ruler. Not all Mongols fled northwards to Mongolia and to those who remained, he promised there would be tolerance and no persecution. He placed the most skilled within his administration. He was also keen to retain the services of the Yuan cavalry forces who were renowned for their fighting skills and so he formed separate Mongol units which remained a feature of the Ming army until its fall in 1644.

A number of reforms were introduced during the early period of Hongwu's rule. As part of his land reform, thousands of peasants were forced to migrate to new areas where they were given land. He also attempted to make his soldiers self-sufficient by giving them plots of land to farm when not fighting. But since much of the land was of poor quality the scheme failed and many soldiers deserted. A similar experiment had also been tried in Tsarist Russia and was equally doomed to failure.

Hongwu attempted a major reform of the civil service. He rewrote the Confucian law code and for a period suspended the civil service examinations. As a strict disciplinarian, he frequently had his most senior scholar-officials executed for incompetency.

Towards the end of his thirty-year reign, as so often happens to those who rule for a relatively long period of time, he feared plots of assassination. Consequently, he formed a personal guard known as the 'Embroidered Uniform Guard' (*Jinyiwei*), named after its distinctive yellow uniform.

The Guard, which remained in force throughout the period of the Ming Dynasty, had the authority to overrule normal judicial proceedings and conduct its own arrests, interrogation and punishments. In practice, it acted as the Emperor's secret service with the right to seek out suspects at all levels of society, including the Imperial family.

Hongwu died in 1398 at the age of 69. He is remembered for his remarkable rise to power, from penniless monk to Emperor of China. By the end of his reign, Hongwu's land reforms resulted in more food which in turn led to a growth in population.

Between 1368 and 1644, sixteen Emperors ruled the Ming dynasty. Over this period of almost three hundred years, the population doubled in size. During this same period, trade was opened up with Western Europe, the Ming embarked upon their own voyages of discovery and the Jesuits began their missionary work in China. And it was during the Ming dynasty that the largest palace complex in the world was constructed.

The Forbidden City

The Forbidden City in Beijing was commissioned by the Yongle Emperor. He was the fourth son of Hongwu and ascended the throne in 1402 after ousting his nephew the Jianwen Emperor.

Yongle moved the capital of the Ming from Nanjing to Beijing. In 1406 he ordered work to begin on what became known as the Forbidden City, which is the English translation for *Zijin Cheng*, meaning 'Purple Forbidden City'.

The complex covers an area of some 190 acres in the centre of Beijing. It consists of 90 palaces and 980 buildings containing almost 9,000 rooms, as well as parks and gardens. The work took 14 years to complete involving over a million labourers.

The gardens are asymmetrical. But in order to induce a sense of harmony, the buildings are all symmetrical in design. The complex is rectangular in shape with a large tower at each corner. Each of its four walls has its own gate, the most important being the Meridian Gate in the South Wall. This gate has five arches, the central arch being reserved for the Emperor's sole use. The only time that the Empress was permitted to pass through the central gate was on her wedding day. The other exception was after the Confucian examinations when the top three scholars were permitted to leave the city through the central gate.

The whole area is surrounded by a moat measuring 6 metres deep and 52 metres wide, as well as an eight metres high wall. The soil from the moat was then used to raise the level of the palace complex giving the impression that it was built on a hill.

All the buildings were built entirely of the highest quality wood from Southwest China, much of which was transported on the Grand Canal. So much wood presented a fire hazard and so giant water cauldrons were placed around the main palaces for use as fire extinguishers.

A unique feature of the building is that they were constructed without the use of any nails. It was believed that nails were incompatible with the natural wood and would destroy the harmony of the structure. Instead of nails, the carpenters used an intricate interlocking method, which is a distinctive feature of many traditional Chinese buildings.

The Forbidden City became a model of Chinese palatial architecture and the style has been copied in cities right across East Asia. It served as the home of emperors and their households, as well as the ceremonial and political centre of Chinese government, for almost 500 years.

Apart from palaces and other buildings, the Imperial city included Taoist and Buddhist temples. Temples for Shamanistic worship were built after 1644 to reflect the needs of the succeeding Manchurian Qing, many of whom followed Shamanism.

In 1860, during the Second Opium War (see Chapter 6), the city was occupied by Anglo-French forces. With the abdication of the last Emperor, Puyi, the Forbidden City became a museum. After the Chinese Civil War in 1949, the Imperial treasures were divided between the Palace Museum in Beijing and the National Palace Museum in Taipei. In 1987, the Forbidden City was declared a World Heritage Site and currently receives some 16 million visitors from across the globe every year.

The Grand Canal

The other great project undertaken by the Ming was the complete renovation of the Grand Canal that was vital for the transport of grain and timber for building the Forbidden City as well as for the movement of troops.

The origins of the Grand Canal go back to the Spring and Autumn Period when King Fuchai of Wu (495-473 BC) constructed a canal linking the Yellow River with the Ji and Huai rivers.

Under the short-lived Sui Dynasty (581-618 AD), the canal underwent a massive dredging programme and new sections were built linking the eastern capital of Luoyang with the western capital of Chang'an.

By the beginning of the fourteenth century, the canal fell into disuse due to neglect by the Yuan. When the Ming came to power and moved the capital from Nanking to Beijing, the economic centre moved and necessitated improved communication links.

The Ming began a complete renovation of the canal including dredging and the construction of new canals, embankments and locks. It is estimated that over 150,000 labourers worked on the renovation and that another 40,000 labourers were needed to maintain the system.

Zheng He: Admiral and Explorer

It was during the Ming period that China's greatest Naval Admiral, Zheng He, embarked upon a series of extensive sea voyages that turned China into a major maritime power.

Zheng He was a Muslim. He was born Ma He in Yunnan in 1371. His father and grandfather had made the pilgrimage to Mecca, becoming *Hajis*, which probably accounted for the fact that Ma He could speak Arabic.

When he was just ten years old, Ma He was captured by the Ming army. He was placed into the service of Zhu Di, who was at that time Prince of Yan, later to become the Yongle Emperor. Soon after he was captured, the boy was castrated, thereby becoming a eunuch and he was given the name Zheng.

Zheng He fought alongside Zhu Di in his campaign to seize the Imperial throne from the Jianwen Emperor. Once Zhu Di ascended the throne as the Yongle Emperor, Zheng He became his favourite palace eunuch. First, he was appointed Grand Director of the Palace and then Chief Envoy to the Imperial Chinese court.

The Yongle Emperor was ambitious for power beyond China. At that time, the Arabs controlled the maritime trade stretching from the Indian Ocean to the Arabian Sea and the Emperor wanted to wrest this power from them. As a trusted servant, an able sailor and efficient administrator, plus the fact that he spoke Arabic, Zheng He was a obvious choice to lead the naval campaign.

In 1405, Zheng He led what was at the time the largest naval expedition in history. The evening before the fleet set sail, the Emperor entertained the whole crew to a sumptuous banquet and presented them all with gifts according to rank. Prayers were also offered to Tienfei, the goddess of sailors.

Most of the fleet's 317 ships had been built at the Dragon Bay shipyard in Nanjing. The largest ship, which was around three times the size of those used by Columbus, measured 440 ft in length and 186 ft in width. It required a crew of 500 men and could carry around 1,000 passengers, including soldiers, interpreters, artisans, doctors and meteorologists.

His ships were known as 'treasure' ships because they were laden with gifts of silks and brocades for foreign rulers. Zheng He was then expected to return with the ships filled with gifts from foreign parts.

The voyages were not simply mercantile, however. Military units were onboard and they were sometimes used to 'encourage' foreign envoys to return with Zheng He to China in order that they could pay homage to the Emperor. In this way, the Yongle Emperor succeeded in bringing large parts of the Indian Ocean, including trading ports in Ceylon, Sumatra and Calicut on the Indian coast, into the Chinese sphere of influence.

During these expeditions, Zheng He was able to rid the Indian Ocean of piracy, including the most infamous pirate, Chen Zuyi, who had plagued the Malacca Straits for years. Chen Zuyi was captured by Zheng He in 1407 and executed in Nanjing.

Over a period of almost thirty years, Zheng He led seven major expeditions to India, Asia, the Middle East and the East coast of Africa. The last expedition took place during the reign of the Xuande Emperor (1424-1425). The great Chinese admiral died in 1433 at the age of about 63.

Although Chinese maritime trade continued after the death of Zheng He, the long-distance expeditions came to an end. Several reasons have been given for this.

First, with the death of the Yongle Emperor, naval exploration lost its patron. At the same time, the eunuchs, who had enjoyed power and privilege under Yongle, lost their influence at Court to the opposing civil service that was favoured by the succeeding Emperor. Furthermore, the Civil Service comprised Confucian scholars who were naturally conservative and inward-looking. Consequently, the scholars disapproved of such overseas ventures which they claimed were too expensive and incompatible with Confucian values.

Another, perhaps more pragmatic reason for the decline of naval exploration, was the need to transfer Imperial resources into defending the northern border against the ongoing threat from the Mongols. This became more urgent when the capital city was moved northwards to Beijing and it necessitated the Ming strengthening the Great Wall.

With the end of the great expeditions, ship building on the same scale ceased and the dockyards fell into disuse. Ships were left to rot and the timber was used for fuel. Men who had previously sailed the seas, now found themselves working as labourers on the Grand Canal. Even the exploits of the great mariner were quietly forgotten. Many records were destroyed and those that survived were filed away until they came to light again in the writings of Liang Qichao (1873-1929), a Chinese scholar, philosopher and reformer.

In recent years, Zheng He's reputation has been resurrected. As part of China's new outward-looking policy and desire to play her part on the world stage, the life of Zheng He and his maritime achievements are now celebrated.

The year 2005 marked the 600th anniversary of the first great naval expedition, To commemorate the event, special books were published and a number of television series aired. The

Chinese Government also built a $50 million museum in Nanjing in honour of Zheng He and his contribution to China's maritime history.

Commentators have observed that Zheng He is being promoted as a foreshadow of China's emergence as a diplomatic, militaristic and commercial player on today's world stage.

European Explorers

Soon after the Chinese abandoned the South Asian seas, the Portuguese took their place. In 1503, the Portuguese explorer Alfonso de Albuquerque secured permission from the King of Kochi, on the Western coast of India, to build a fortress for use as a trading post. This marked the foundation of the Portuguese Empire in the East.

In 1510, Albuquerque conquered Goa and the following year he launched a campaign, with a force of around 1200 men and eighteen ships, to take Malacca. Despite opposition from the local Muslim population, he succeeded in erecting a fortress.

However, at the time, Malacca was a tributary state of China, having earlier been subdued by Zheng He. When news of the Portuguese invasion of Malacca arrived at the Ming court, China's response was swift. All Portuguese diplomats and many Portuguese traders were immediately imprisoned. Twenty-three were tortured to death. The rest languished in prison where many more died.

By 1553, relations between the Ming and the Portuguese had improved and the Europeans were given permission to anchor, but not settle, in Macau. They were, however, allowed to build storehouses on land so that they could dry out their goods in the rainy season.

Since the reduction of the Chinese Navy, pirates had become a serious problem and the Portuguese helped the Ming clear the seas around Macau. In Return, in 1557, the Portuguese were granted the right to permanent settlement on the island in exchange for an annual sum of 500 *taels* (41.6 lbs of silver). Full sovereignty of Macau did not return to China until December 1999.

Matteo Ricci

Once the Portuguese were in Macau it was not long before the Vatican began sending Jesuit priests to the East with a mission to preach the Gospel to the Chinese.

The first to arrive was the Italian Jesuit Matteo Ricci who was born in 1552 in Macerata which was then part of the Papal States. Ricci had studied under the renowned German astronomer and Jesuit priest, Christopher Clavius. By the time Ricci applied for a missionary post, he was proficient in theology, philosophy, mathematics, cosmology and astronomy.

In 1578, Ricci arrived in Goa, where he spent some time teaching and preaching. In 1582, he had reached Macau and immediately embarked upon the task of learning the Chinese script, language and culture.

Macau was to be the launching pad for Jesuit missionaries to mainland China. In 1583 Ricci travelled to the mainland with another Jesuit Priest named Michele Ruggieri. The two men spent some time in Guangzhou, northwest of today's Hong Kong.

It is thought that whilst in Guangzhou, in around the year 1584, Ricci produced the first Chinese map of the World, known in Chinese as *Da Ying Quan Tu*, literally meaning 'Complete Map of the Great World'. The map was a woodcut, measuring 5 ft. high and 12 ft. wide. It placed China at the centre of the world and used Chinese characters, to describe other continents.

The original map disappeared. However, in 1602, an improved and expanded version, known as *Kunyu Wanguo Quantu* (A Map of the Myriad Countries of the World'), was made and six copies of this map, produced on rice paper, still survive. Currently copies are held in the Vatican Apostolic Library Collection and the James Ford Bell Library at the University of Minnesota, as well as Kyoto University in Japan. It is not thought that any copy exists in China itself.

It was not long before Matteo Ricci's exceptional skills in cosmology and astronomy came to the attention of the Ming court and in 1601 he was invited to be an adviser to the Wanli Emperor (1572-1620).

Ricci was to be the first westerner ever to enter the Forbidden City. However, he never did have a face to face meeting with the Emperor because by this time, although the Emperor was interested in Western thought on astronomy and cosmology, he was living a life of virtual seclusion.

While in Beijing, Matteo Ricci succeeded in converting several senior officials to Christianity and he was given permission to build Beijing's first Roman Catholic Church, today's Cathedral of the Immaculate Conception. Part of his success was probably due to his ability to present Christianity in a way that was accessible to the Chinese people. For example, he had mastered the Chinese language and customs and he habitually wore Mandarin dress. He was also well-versed in Confucian classics and he used many Confucian terms in his preaching and teaching. Not surprisingly, Ricci's policy of inculturation was frowned on by both Chinese and Christian conservatives.

Chinese Ceramics

China had been developing its ceramics industry for many centuries, but it was during the Ming dynasty that Chinese porcelain found its way onto the European market.

Some of the first pieces to be exported were referred to as Kraak porcelain, named after the Portuguese ships called carracks, that were used for transportation. In 1602 and in 1604, two of these carracks, the *San Yago* and *Santa Catarina*, were captured by the Dutch. The cargo, including valuable porcelain, was auctioned off in the Netherlands, with some of the most valuable pieces being sold to the Kings of England and France.

Eventually, the Dutch East India Company became the main transporter of Chinese pottery to Europe and orders began flowing into China for specific designs. While many of the earlier pieces remained faithful to the blue on white colour scheme, the designs on porcelain for the European market omitted the symbolism that was prevalent on pottery for the Chinese market. In time, more extravagant colouring became popular as well as the depiction of European family crests and coats of arms. The popularity and prevalence of Chinese porcelain can be seen in many contemporary Dutch paintings.

Chinese production of ceramics was disrupted around 1620 with the death of the Wanli Emperor. The political turmoil that followed his death caused many of the kilns to close down. With Chinese supplies being unavailable, the Dutch potteries in the Delft region of the Netherlands started to make their own copies.

While initially the preserve of the wealthy, later ceramics gradually became more accessible. Today, the 'Ming Vase' remains a valuable item and many Europeans are proud possessors of 'China' dinner sets that are kept in display cabinets, being too precious for every-day use.

Conclusion

The Ming dynasty marked something of a watershed in Chinese history in several respects. The early years formed a period of transition from the Mongol led Yuan to the return of an ethnic Han dynasty. During the same period, Beijing became the capital city and the Forbidden City was built in the form that we see it today. The first Chinese voyages of exploration were undertaken, the first Jesuit priests arrived and trade in Chinese ceramics flourished.

The Ming came to power at a time of natural disaster and a corrupt Yuan government which led to social unrest and rebellion. At the time, there was also a powerful sense of millenarianism as espoused by the White Lotus Society.

The first emperor of the Ming, Hongwu, was a powerful and pragmatic ruler. Above all, having been born into poverty, he understood the needs of the people. At the same time, his own struggle in early life, had taught him the importance of good leadership.

Although much of the Mongol leadership returned to Mongolia when the Yuan lost power, the Hongwu Emperor wisely invited the most skilled to join his administration. Even more important, was the need to maintain Mongol military power and special Mongol units remained loyal to the Ming dynasty throughout its rule.

The Yongle Emperor usurped the throne when he came to power in 1402 and it is thought that his decision to move the capital from Nanjing to Beijing and then build the Forbidden City, was a conscious attempt to cement his Imperial authority.

The Forbidden City was, and remains, the largest palace complex in the world and its unique style of architecture spread quickly across East Asian countries. The need at the time to transport vast amounts of precious timber for its construction was one reason for the upgrading of the Grand Canal.

The Yongle Emperor was an extremely ambitious ruler. Not only did he usurp the throne and build the greatest palace complex on earth, but he also sought to extend his power beyond the shores of China. He achieved this through his patronage of Zheng He who had risen through the ranks of the Palace Eunochs.

Under the leadership of Zheng He, China extended her influence across the seas of India to the Arabian Gulf, making tributary states of kingdoms such as Sumatra and Malacca in the process. However, apart from one last voyage under the Xuande Emperor, these great voyages of exploration essentially came to an end at the beginning of the 15th Century with the deaths of the Yongle Emperor and also Zheng He.

There were two main reasons for the ending of China's ambitious maritime ventures. First, opposition was growing from the Confucian scholars who claimed that the voyages were both too expensive and contrary to the spirit of Confucionism.The more likely reason, however, was the need to transfer resources from the sea to the North in order to defend the Empire against the Mongols.

The retreat of the Chinese from the South Indian seas coincided with the arrival of the European explorers. The Portuguese were the first to arrive and settle in Goa on the West coast of India. Jesuit priests soon followed, the best-known being Matteo Ricci, a respected astronomer. Ricci's 'Complete Map of the Great World' was to be a valuable Western contribution to the Chinese.

The Portuguese were followed by the Dutch and it was the Dutch who began the transportation of Chinese ceramics to Europe. When Chinese production was disrupted, the Dutch began making their own copies of Chinese porcelain.

The Ming dynasty was a high point in Chinese cultural flowering. It was also a period of openness and it was outward-looking. As a measure of its productivity, the population doubled over the 300 years of Ming rule. With its fall, China once more turned inwards on itself.

The Ming were ethnically Han and they were sandwiched between two non-Han Dynasties: the Mongol-led Yuan and their successors, the Manchurian-led Qing. The Qing came to power in 1636 and would rule until 1912 when Imperial China became the Republic of China.

*****

CHAPTER SIX

The Manchu Conquest

The Manchu

The last Empire of China was ruled by the Qing dynasty who were ethnic Manchu, from Manchuria. The term Manchuria was first used during the 17th Century to describe the north-eastern region of China. Once the Qing came to power in 1644, the Chinese referred to the region as the three Eastern Provinces. Today the region comprises the provinces of Heilongjiang, Jilin and Liaoning.

The Manchus were descendants of the Jurchens, who had ruled China briefly as the Jin Dynasty between 1115 and 1234. (see Chapter Four)

Unlike the Mongols, who were nomadic, the Manchu were settled agriculturalists. Today they make up the fourth largest ethnic group in China.

The Rise of the Qing

The 'Transition from Ming to Qing', also referred to as the 'Manchu Conquest of the Han', took place over several decades. The Manchu tribes had been vassals of the Ming and in 1616 one particular tribal chief, Nurhaci of the Manchu Aisin Gioro clan, succeeded in uniting a number of the tribes under his leadership. He was then elected Khan of the 'Later Jin Dynasty'.

In 1618, Nurhaci drew up a list of 'Seven Grievances' against the Ming and encouraged the other tribes to rebel. He organised them into 'Eight Banners' putting all Manchu families under one particular administrative/military 'banner'.

When Nurhaci died in 1626, he was succeeded by his son, Hong Taiji. Hong Taiji took the title Emperor rather than Khan and renamed the 'Later Jin Dynasty' the 'Qing' dynasty.

As Hong Taiji's power grew, an increasing number of Ming generals defected and joined the Qing. Because the Manchu were outnumbered by the Han by a hundred to one, he introduced policies aimed at integrating the Han and ethnic Mongols with the Qing. He incorporated them into the 'Banner' system and rewarded senior Ming officers by permitting them to keep their military rank and giving them Qing princesses as wives and concubines.

To further help integration, he encouraged mixed marriages and at one point organised the mass marriage of 1,000 couples uniting Han Chinese officers with Manchu women. Mixed marriages were later to be banned however.

Having strengthened his army with Han and Mongol troops, Hong Taiji was able to consolidate Qing power and conquer more territory in Mongolia and Korea. More crucially, he was now in a position to consolidate his power over the Ming.

The Conquest of China

When Hong Taiji died in 1643, there followed a power struggle among his many sons. A compromise was reached whereby the five-year old Shunzhi Emperor succeeded to the throne under the co-regency of Hong Taiji's 16th son Dorgan. It was to be Dorgan who led the final conquest of China.

Early in 1644, a disaffected peasant army attacked Beijing. They burned down the palace of the Forbidden City and for several days ran riot: looting, murdering and raping women. In despair, the Ming emperor hanged himself on a hill just outside the city.

Dorgan capitalised on the situation and offered to help the Ming leadership fight off the rebels. His offer was accepted by the Ming and his forces attacked the peasant army at Shanhai Pass on the 27th May 1644.

The battle, known as the Battle of Shanhai Pass, ended with a resounding victory for Dorgan and he went on to claim the city of Beijing for the Qing dynasty. While he ordered that there should be no looting by his troops, he executed all Ming claimants to the throne. He then announced that all Ming officers who surrendered to the Qing, would be allowed to keep their positions.

At the same time, Dorgan humiliated Han males by ordering them to change their hairstyles. Instead of the traditional long hair tied in a bun, they were forced to shave the front of their heads and grow a *queue*, or long pigtail in the Manchu style.

There was great opposition to the Manchu hairstyle. Resistance was widespread and resulted in between 75,000 and 100,000 Han males being executed. In 1645, a further massacre of those resisting Qing rule took place in Yangzhou. Exact numbers of those who died are not known but a figure of 800,000 is often cited.

The Kangxi Emperor and 'High Qing'

It took another forty years, with the death of hundreds of thousands of lives, to put down all opposition to the Qing. Consolidation was finally achieved under the Kangxi Emperor who came to power in 1662. He reigned until 1722, making him the longest ruling Emperor in Chinese history.

Kangxi's rule marks the beginning of the 'High Qing' period. Apart from quelling dissent in Southern China and on the island of Taiwan, he succeeded in thwarting Russia's territorial ambitions in the Amur River region of Northeast China. Kangxi also brought Tibet and parts of Central Asia into China's sphere of influence, making the Qing period the largest in terms of territory in Chinese history.

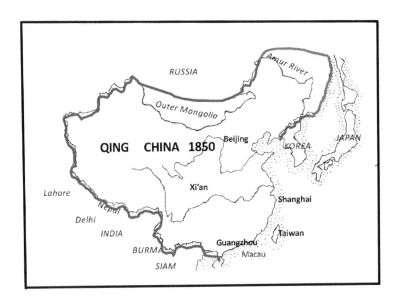

Among his greatest challenges was how to find a way to unite the majority Han with the various minority groups, including the Manchu people. One way to achieve this was to invite Han scholars to work on his new Kangxi Dictionary. In this way the scholars gradually became more involved in state affairs.

The Kangxi Emperor, as his predecessor, Hong Taiji, disliked certain Han practices. In particular, the Manchu found the Han tradition of foot binding distasteful.

Foot binding had been introduced during the Song Dynasty (960-1279). Initially only practiced by the aristocracy, by the Qing period, females of all levels of Han society bound their feet. Small feet were considered beautiful, even erotic.

Girls as young as five would undergo the painful process of having their toes broken and their feet tightly bound in bandages. Over a period of time the bandages would be tightened even further, the aim being to reduce the size of the foot to just four inches, known as the 'lotus foot'. Despite the fact that such disfigurement caused great pain and often led to infection, many women were still able to walk reasonable distances and even work in the fields.

By the 19th Century, some 50% of all Han Chinese women, including 100% of the upper classes, had bound feet. This was partly because the 'lotus foot' was more likely to procure a good marriage. By this time, however, opposition was steadily growing, especially from women's groups and Christian missionary organisations.

It was not until 1912 that foot binding was officially banned by the new Republic of China when foot inspectors were appointed to tour the country. Despite all efforts, elderly women with bound feet could still be found in remote regions as late as 1950. The last factory manufacturing 'lotus' shoes was closed down in 1999.

British Trade Delegation: 1793

By the 17th Century, China had the highest GDP in the world and a population of over 13 million. Apart from being totally self-sufficient, the country earned a vast income from exports. To satisfy Europe's insatiable appetite for silk, porcelain and especially tea, shiploads of goods sailed from China to European ports. But this created a trade imbalance which caused concern, particularly with the British.

The British East India Company was already well established in India. However, in China all foreign traders were confined to a small enclave in Canton (modern Guangzhou), known as 'The Factories'. Their goods were held in warehouses and all foreign traders were restricted to working with local merchants known as the Hong. The British Government wanted to break out of this system and gain access to new trading ports. They decided to send a trade delegation to meet the Chinese Emperor with the aim of securing official trading rights in mainland China.

In 1793, King George III sent a large delegation, led by George, Lord Macartney, to meet the Qianlong Emperor. Before being offered an audience, lengthy negotiations took place regarding correct protocol. Chinese and British accounts of the negotiations differ. The British accounts say that Macartney refused to make the traditional *kowtow* to the Emperor, claiming that he was representing the King of England and that kneeling and touching the ground with his forehead was beneath his status and the dignity of an English gentleman. The Chinese accounts, on the other hand, state that he agreed to *kowtow*, albeit with some reluctance.

It was not a good start to the first meeting between the Emperor of China and a representative of the English crown. Then there were further tensions over the question of gifts. Macartney arrived with chests full of expensive items but they were received by Qianlong indifferently, taken as tribute from a vassal, rather than gifts from a ruler of equal standing.

The offerings were intended to convince the Chinese of the innovative and scientific value of British goods in the hope that the Emperor would consider importing them. But he simply remarked that China did not need to import anything, because his country had all it needed. Consequently, the British came away with no trade deal and her gifts had been spurned.

The failure of Macartney's embassy was initially blamed on his refusal to *kowtow,* but on closer examination of the exchange of letters between the Emperor and George III, the problem was exacerbated by communication and cultural differences.

While the mission failed to get the desired trade concessions, the British had gained valuable information regarding China's military power and they also had a greater understanding of her culture.

But the problem of a trade imbalance remained and would not be redressed until the Chinese started importing British goods. There was, however, one commodity that was becoming increasingly popular among the Chinese and that was opium.

The First Opium War: 1839-1842

Opium production had been officially banned by the Chinese government in 1729 but by the beginning of the 19th Century, opium consumption, which was initially confined to the aristocracy, was beginning to spread to all levels of society, along with its consequent addiction.

The British East India Company already grew the crop in India, where the opium trade was legal. Despite the fact that the Emperor refused to legalise it in China, the British began transporting ship loads of opium to privateers off the Chinese coast. The opium would then be transferred onto local boats and taken to the mainland. As a result, Chinese silver began to fill British coffers, so helping to redress the balance of trade.

Faced with this illegal trade in drugs and the growing addiction problem, in 1839 the Daoguang Emperor appointed Viceroy Lin Zexu to deal with the situation. Zexu first arrested around 1,700 opium dealers and confiscated 70,000 opium pipes. He then confiscated over 20,000 chests of opium; he confined the foreign traders to Canton and blocked their supplies.

While the British government recognised China's right to ban the trade in opium, it was critical of the way that the traders of Canton had been treated. They had been offered no compensation for the loss of their goods and that by blocking supplies to Canton, the traders faced potential starvation.

Consequently, it was decided to send British naval ships to Chinese waters in order to 'protect' its citizens trapped in Canton. After months of what is termed 'gunboat diplomacy', some skirmishes and Britain's threat to attack Nanking, the Chinese finally capitulated.

The Treaty of Nanking: 1842

On the 29th August, 1842, Britain's representative Sir Henry Pottinger met with three representatives of the Qing Emperor on HMS Cornwallis that was anchored off Nanking. Here they signed the Treaty of Nanking. In October of the same year the Treaty was ratified by the Daoguang Emperor of China and Victoria, Queen of the United Kingdom of Great Britain and Ireland.

The Treaty covered four main areas: trading rights, war reparations, amnesties and the future of Hong Kong. Under the terms, the restrictions on the Canton system were lifted and the monopoly of the Hong merchants was ended. At the same time, Britain secured four new ports. They were known as Treaty Ports and one was Shanghai. It was also agreed that the British would be permitted to trade directly with local Chinese merchants rather than go through agents such as the Hong merchants of Canton.

The Chinese were to pay the British an amount of six million silver dollars as compensation for lost opium and a further twelve million silver dollars in war reparations. Once the first payment towards war reparations had been made, it was agreed that the British would withdraw her troops and all prisoners should be released.

In 1846, Christian missionaries were permitted to settle in the Treaty Ports. Despite being officially banned from the rest of China, the missionaries still managed to penetrate the vast interior with the Gospel message and Western ideas.

Finally, Hong Kong was ceded as a Crown Colony in perpetuity to Queen Victoria. In 1860, the Kowloon Peninsula was combined with the territory of Hong Kong. Thirty years later, in 1898, the area was further extended and became known as the New Territories. At this point the 'perpetuity' clause was changed into a 99-year lease and in 1997 all land that fell under the lease was transferred to the People's Republic of China.

The Second Opium War: 1856-1860

The Second Opium War, sometimes referred to as the 'Arrow War', in reference to the incident concerning the ship named Arrow that sparked off the hostilities, started in 1856.

Tensions were running high by this time because the British felt that the Treaty of Nanking, known as the first of the 'Unequal Treaties', failed to satisfy the aims of the British, largely because it did not result in increased trade. Furthermore, diplomatic relations were worsening, with attacks on foreigners becoming commonplace.

Britain wanted to renegotiate the Treaty of Nanking. She wanted more Treaty Ports, exemption from internal duties and foreigners to be given free access to the whole of China. There were also further demands for legislation on what was known as the coolie trade.

In 1807, the United States, Great Britain and Ireland had abolished the international slave trade. Since it then became unlawful to transport African slaves, unskilled labour from China became a substitute.

Officially the coolies were free men who volunteered for the work and signed a contract of between two and five years. The reality was that very few understood what they were signing up to. They were human cargo being trafficked by unscrupulous 'go-between' men.

The coolies were transported, mainly to America, in slave-like conditions that resulted in a fatality rate of up to 40%. Those who survived the journey often died before the end of their contract. Hundreds of thousands of Chinese men (they were not accompanied by women and children in contrast to the African slave trade) were transported to work on plantations, railroads and in mines.

Since the British also benefited from the trade, they wanted to protect their interests by having proper legislation regarding the coolie trade put in place.

Outbreak of hostilities

In October 1856, the Chinese navy seized a cargo vessel named the *Arrow* and imprisoned its crew, assuming it was a pirate ship. While the vessel was originally a pirate ship, it had subsequently been sold to the British and was flying the British flag. The British initially responded with punitive action against Chinese forts in the Pearl River but open warfare soon broke out.

Britain invited America and Russia to join in a coalition against China on the grounds that they shared common grievances. Both countries initially rejected the invitation but then France agreed to join Britain. France's decision was influenced by the public outcry over the execution by the Chinese of a French missionary named Auguste Chapdelaine.

The pace of war increased towards the end of 1857 with up to 170 British ships being sent to the area. Furthermore, after the British succeeded in putting down the Indian Uprising in 1857, and with the end of the Crimean War, more troops were available for the war in China, which substantially added to the number of British forces.

Treaties of Tianjin and Aigun: June 1858

Hostilities stopped briefly while negotiating the Treaties of Taijin and Aigun. Under the terms of the Treaties, Britain, France, Russia and America were to be permitted embassies in Peking (today's Beijing) together with the right for foreign residents to be tried in their own courts rather than under Chinese Law. Ten more Chinese ports were acquired together with free navigation along the Yangtze River. Foreigners would no longer be banned from travelling anywhere in China and the Qing government was to pay further indemnities to Britain and France.

The Treaty of Aigun dealt with the Russia/Chinese border. Russia gained territory that under the Nerchinsk Treaty of 1689, had been made part of China. Russia acquired even more territory in 1860 under the Convention of Peking that allowed the Russians to build the city of Vladivostock.

Burning of the Summer Palaces

There was opposition from the traditionalists in the Qing court to both Treaties and pressure was put upon the Xianfeng Emperor to reject the terms and fight back. As a result, Xianfeng failed to ratify the Treaties, choosing instead to invite the British representatives to further negotiations.

However, the meeting did not go well. The British envoy, Harry Parkes, was accused of insulting the Qing ambassador and things got out of control. Parkes and his companions were arrested, imprisoned and tortured in the traditional Chinese manner. Parkes escaped the torture but most of his men, numbering around thirty, died as a result of the *tourniquet*. This was a method whereby hands and feet were tied together behind the back so tightly that the limbs were eventually severed from the body and the victim suffered a slow death.

When news of the atrocities reached England, there was a public outcry and angry voices in Parliament called for military action against the Chinese.

Hostilities resumed in June 1859. On the 6th October 1860, after defeating some 10,000 Qing troops, a joint Anglo-French force entered Beijing. The 30 years old Xianfeng Emperor fled the imperial palace leaving his 27 years old younger brother, Prince Gong, to negotiate peace terms.

The Anglo-French forces looted the two Summer Palaces, both of which contained valuable treasures. Two precious staves of office, made of gold and green jade-stone, were reserved as gifts; one for Queen Victoria and the other for Emperor Napoleon III. Queen Victoria also received a little dog that was rescued from an elderly concubine who had been unable to flee. Five little Pekinese dogs were transported to England at the time and became the origin of the Pekinese breed outside China.

On the 18th October, Lord Elgin, Commander of the British troops, ordered the burning of the Summer Palaces. He decided that the destruction of the Imperial Palace in the Forbidden City would be unwise and could hinder peace negotiations. His aim was to show that the treatment of British citizens in such a barbaric manner would not be tolerated and the burning of the Summer Palaces would send the right warning. The French played no part in the burning and it took hundreds of British troops to light the blazes needed to set the palaces alight. The flames burned for three days while a heavy black smoke hung over the city.

Having suffered a decisive military defeat, plus the humiliation of watching the destruction of two ancient palaces, Prince Gong was forced to sign the Treaties of Tianjin and Aigun. He had been chosen by the Emperor to deal with the foreigners because he was more open to foreign negotiations than his elder brother. Prince Gong remained in Beijing and established a reasonable working relationship with the Embassies.

The Xianfeng Emperor, on the other hand, could not bring himself to meet face to face with any of the foreigners, or even remain in the city of Beijing. So he travelled with his family and entourage to his hunting lodge beyond the Great Wall. Although the lodge was vast, it was not as comfortable as the Forbidden City. Also, it was cold and not really fit for habitation during the cold North China winter months.

The Emperor caught a cold from which he never recovered. On the 22nd August 1861, he died in his hunting lodge. He was just coming up to 31 years. He left one son, Zaichun, who was born to Imperial Concubine Lady Lan. Since the boy was just five years, a regency was appointed. It consisted of the inner circle of the Qing court who were all hard-line traditionalists. The young Emperor's mother, Lady Lan, was elevated to the status of Empress Dowager Cixi and when Zaichun came of age, he ruled as the Tongzhi Emperor.

DATE	EMPEROR	EVENT
1793	Qianlong	MacCartney Trade Delegation
1839	Daoguang	First Opium War
1850	Daoguang	Taiping Rebellion
1852	Xianfeng	Cixi becomes Concubine of Xianfeng
1856	Xianfeng	Second Opium War
1864	Cixi	End of Taiping Rebellion

The Taiping Rebellion: 1850-1864

Just before the outbreak of the Second Opium War, the Qing dynasty was faced with a serious grass roots uprising. The causes were various, including a series of natural disasters, economic stagnation, population growth and the effects of the Unequal Treaties that contributed to a rise in opium addiction.

The leader of the rebellion was Hong Xiuquan, a Han Chinese who was born into the *Hakka* tribe in the southern region of present-day Guangzhou. He was a studious child and hoped to enter the prestigious Civil Service. But despite several attempts to pass the stiff Confucian Entrance Examinations, he failed and this was to have a profound influence on his decisions in later life.

When Hong was about 23, after failing the examination for the third time, he had a nervous breakdown with bouts of delirium that lasted for several days. When he recovered, he claimed to have received a vision whereby he had visited heaven and met his celestial family.

When Hong failed the examinations for the fourth and last time, he became totally disillusioned with the Confucian Civil Service and the Qing establishment. At this point he began reading Christian literature that he had been given by American Baptist missionaries. He then became convinced that he was the younger brother of Jesus and that he had a divine mission to reform society and defeat Manchu 'demonism'.

Hong destroyed the Confucian books and Buddhist idols in his home. He then started preaching his own syncretistic religion which was a mix of Christianity and Chinese folk lore.

When he was about 33, Hong became leader of a group called the God Worshipping Society which had a religious, political and nationalistic agenda. In 1847, he started work on a Bible, known as the *Authorised Taiping Version of the Bible.*

Thousands of disaffected Han peasants converted to Hong's form of 'Christianity' and the number of Taiping grew to around 20,000. The organisation was highly militaristic. On the 11th January 1851, the rebel army defeated a much smaller force of 7,000 Qing at Jintian, a town in today's Guiping.

In the wake of this victory, Hong Xiuquan, claimed the title Heavenly King of the Taiping Heavenly Kingdom and in 1853 he made Nanking, the old capital of the Ming dynasty, the Taiping capital city. He then began to systematically destroy all Buddhist and Taoist temples in the city.

With the help of his cousin Hong Rengan, who had also studied with the Protestant missionaries in Hong Kong, the Heavenly King began a series of reforms.

Fundamental to his new policy was a rejection of the Confucian classics in favour of the Bible, together with class and gender equality. Foot binding was banned, as was opium, alcohol, gambling, concubinage, prostitution and slavery. The Manchu hairstyle, the *queue,* was ordered to be replaced by long, loose hair, often tied with a red band.

The most controversial of Hong's policies, however, was the forced separation of the sexes. Between 1851 and 1855 this ruling even applied to married couples.

After taking Jintian, Hong's forces moved northwards towards Shanghai, destroying towns and villages and murdering thousands of innocent people. As news of the atrocities reached Shanghai, the Chinese population deserted the city. The foreigners in Shanghai braced themselves and put their ships on alert. The problem for the foreigners at the time was a lack of reliable information. It was only later that the seriousness of the rebellion became apparent.

Britain initially adopted a policy of neutrality towards the Taiping but this proved unpopular at home. Since the rebels were ostensibly 'Christian', a large proportion of the British public believed that Britain should intervene on their behalf against a despotic imperial power that had committed atrocities against British citizens. This was also the view of the American and British missionaries based in Hong Kong.

By 1856, the Taiping were beginning to show signs of weakness due to infighting. Their real downfall, however, came at the hands of the 'Ever Victorious Army' which was an Imperial force trained and led by Europeans. It was to be the first Chinese army to employ modern methods of warfare and became the model for all later Chinese military.

One of the key commanders of the Ever Victorious Army was Charles George Gordon, a British Army Officer, who had previously served in the Crimea and was later to be killed in the Sudan, where he was known as Gordon of Khartoum. In 1860, Gordon volunteered to serve in China and was initially sympathetic towards the Taiping. However, when he witnessed at first hand the devastation and atrocities committed in Shanghai, he changed his allegiance. In recognition of his contribution towards the defeat of the Taiping, he was known as Chinese Gordon.

The fourteen-year civil war between the Qing and the Taiping affected virtually all regions of the country, bringing some 30 million Chinese under Hong's rule. It resulted in an estimated 20-60 million dead, with 100 million people displaced, many of whom sought refuge in Hong Kong. It is said to have been one of the bloodiest wars in history and the greatest conflict of the 19th Century.

Conclusion

The Manchu conquest of China that began in 1636, caused hundreds of thousands of deaths and widespread devastation. It took almost forty years to bring the entire country under Qing control. The next challenge facing the new Qing dynasty, was to find a way of integrating the minority Manchu rulers with the majority Han and other minority groups.

The years under the Kangxi Emperor (1662-1722), marked the beginning of the 'High Qing' period. It was a time when the Empire was at its greatest extent in terms of territory and had the highest GDP in the world.

China's wealth stemmed from the fact that the country was totally self-sufficient and also earned an enormous income through the exportation to Europe of silk, porcelain and especially tea. This resulted in a trade imbalance. While vast amounts of silver filled Chinese coffers, European traders went away empty handed.

Consequently, Britain and to a lesser extent, America, France and Russia, sent trade delegations to China hoping to secure concessions from the Qing Empire. The delegations were initially a failure due to the totally different worldview of China compared to the rest of the world.

For most of its history, China had adopted an isolationist policy, seeing itself as holding 'the Mandate of Heaven' and being the centre of the 'universe'. She viewed foreign nations as vassal states rather than countries of equal standing. Therefore, when the British delegation presented the Emperor with gifts as a sign of friendship, he received them with indifference, viewing the gifts as tribute from a vassal state. This, along with the general treatment of the trade delegation, led Britain to seek an alternative way of redressing the trade balance.

Knowing there was a market for opium, Britain and America began the illegal importation of the drug. The Emperor asked the Europeans to cease the importation. When his appeals were ignored he ordered the destruction of vast amounts of opium that were held in British warehouses and he put an embargo on food supplies to the European enclave at Canton.

In 1839 hostilities broke out, marking the beginning of the Opium Wars between Britain and China. A Peace Treaty was signed in 1842, resulting in the British acquisition of five Treaty Ports including Shanghai and Hong Kong was ceded as a Crown Colony. Despite the concessions made by the Chinese in 1842, the British remained dissatisfied and a Second Opium War broke out in 1856.

Peace negotiations, aimed at ending the war, went disastrously wrong and resulted in the imprisonment and torture of members of the British delegation. Public outcry and fierce parliamentary debate led the British government to order a swift response. The Summer Palaces were burned down and the Qing were forced to sign a second Treaty that was even more humiliating for the Chinese than that of 1842.

The grassroots Taiping Rebellion against the Qing, that broke out in 1850, gained momentum in the wake of the devastation caused by the Opium Wars. While Hong Xiuquan's early followers were drawn to his 'Christian' message, the majority of the Taiping recruits were homeless, poverty-stricken peasants and casualties of the ongoing wars.

Because the Taiping claimed to be 'Christian', Western powers, and particularly the Protestant missionary organisations, were initially sympathetic to the rebel cause and considered offering them military support against the Qing. But when it became apparent that the Taiping was a syncretistic cult that massacred innocent people, thoughts of support were withdrawn.

While the Taiping Rebellion dragged on until 1864, the Second Opium War officially ended in 1860. The signing of the Peace Treaty with Britain significantly changed the relationship between the two powers. The Qing were no longer viewed as an enemy, but as a trade partner. Furthermore, it was a trade partner that was being weakened because of the ongoing Taiping Rebellion.

It was therefore in Britain's interest to come to the aid of the Qing and offer military assistance. The Crimean War had ended in 1856 and the Indian Uprising in 1857, thus releasing British troops available for China. Although the Taiping had been showing signs of weakness since 1856, it was British military help that contributed to the ending of the rebellion in 1860.

After centuries of isolationism, in the 19th Century China was forced to open her doors to the world. The Peace Treaties of 1842 and 1860 benefitted Britain and other foreign powers at the expense of the Chinese. They are referred to as the 'Unequal Treaties' because China lost so much of her sovereignty.

The beginning of the 19th Century was not just a turning point in Chinese history; it marked the beginning of 'A Hundred Years of Humiliation' that is still very much in the Chinese consciousness.

*****

CHAPTER SEVEN

The Last Empire

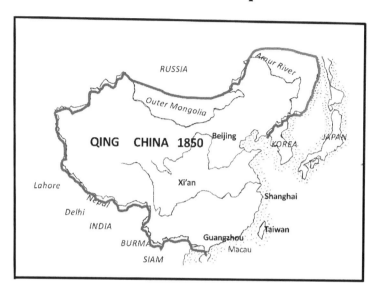

When the British burned down the Old Summer Palace in 1860, the Xianfeng Emperor fled to the Forbidden City in Beijing. Then, when faced with a humiliating defeat, he abandoned Beijing and travelled with his family to his hunting lodge beyond the Great Wall, where he died in August 1861.

Xianfeng was just thirty years old when he died. He was succeeded by his only son, five-year old Zaichun. Later to be known as the Tongzhi Emperor, the boy was the son of the Emperor's concubine named Xingzhen, better known as Cixi.

Cixi

Cixi was born in November 1835 into an aristocratic Manchu family. Her father was a government employee and in the early years she had a carefree childhood. Being a Manchu, she had escaped the torture of foot binding. Although she received a good education for a girl of her standing, this did not include the classics or written Chinese. Consequently, she has often been described as semi-literate.

While not educated in the strict sense, Cixi's resourcefulness and intelligence became apparent when she was about eleven years old. At this time the Opium Wars were causing economic hardship across China and Cixi's family, along with most of the population, suffered as a result. Apparently Cixi showed exceptional resourcefulness by organising the sale of the family's household goods and taking in sewing jobs to bring in extra income.

In March 1852, Cixi was ordered to attend the Forbidden Palace. Along with hundreds of other aristocratic Manchu girls, she was to be presented to the Emperor as a potential consort. Attendance was obligatory and only if she had been rejected by the Emperor, either as a concubine for himself, or for one of the princes, would she be permitted to return home and marry someone of her choice.

The girls were ordered to wear simple clothes and were not required to *kowtow* in order that the Emperor could see their faces clearly. Beauty was not a priority. A girl was chosen for her dignity, gracefulness and modesty. Above all she had to be refined and able to fit into court life.

Cixi was one of the chosen eight. The favourite became the first consort, known as Empress C'ian. Cixi came lower in rank at number six. Each consort was given quarters, food rations and servants according to her rank. But when the Taiping Rebellion began to drain the Government treasury, the palace expenses had to be reduced, including the clothing and food allowance of the concubines.

The young Emperor was ill-equipped to face the devastating Opium Wars, as well as the Taiping rebellion, so early in his reign. He was physically frail due to a premature birth and a fall from a horse left him with a limp. He held violent anti-Western feelings after having witnessed his father's humiliation when forced to sign the Treaty of Nanking. It was Xianfeng's antipathy towards foreigners that led the Emperor to choose him as successor to the throne, despite the fact that he was only fourth in line of succession.

Cixi was well aware of the Emperor's anxieties and she understood the political situation. But she made the mistake of speaking to the Emperor about affairs of the state, so crossing the boundary of her role as concubine. This infuriated the Emperor and he called on Empress C'ian, who was responsible for the behaviour of all the consorts, to do something about it; by getting rid of Cixi if necessary.

But Empress C'ian liked Cixi and pleaded with the Emperor on her behalf, promising that she would deal with the situation. This became the beginning of a life-long, close friendship between the two women.

The Coup

As a concubine, Cixi was not recognised as the official mother of her son, who ascended the throne as the Tongzhi Emperor. Instead, tradition dictated that the child was put into the care of Empress C'ian, who became Dowager Empress on the death of the Emperor.

The situation could have led to problems between the two young women, who were only in their twenties. But as they were close friends, they schemed together to find a way of changing Cixi's status to that of Dowager Empress. They succeeded by citing a precedent that went back two hundred years, to 1662, when there were two Dowager Empresses following the death of Emperor Kangxi.

Just before he died, Emperor Xianfeng appointed a Council of hard-line, anti-Western Regents to rule on behalf of the young Emperor. Many in the Court, including the two Dowager Empresses and other members of the royal family, believed that the Regents were holding China back from progress. They would have preferred Prince Gong, who was pro-modernisation and open to western trade, to have been made Regent. Furthermore, he had already proven his suitability when he negotiated with the foreign powers that led to the signing of the peace treaties.

In October 1861, just two months after the death of Xianfeng, Cixi succeeded in engineering a coup against the Council of Regents. On trumped up charges, the most senior of the Regents were executed while the remainder were sent to remote regions across the Empire. It was then proclaimed publicly that all state matters would be decided upon by the two Dowager Empresses in the name of the young Emperor Tongzhi. Decisions would then be passed for action to Prince Gong, who was appointed Grand Adviser.

From then on, the two Dowager Empresses rose between five and six am each morning in order to be ready to meet government officials. Throughout the proceedings the two women spoke from behind a yellow screen, while the young Emperor sat on a throne in front of the screen. Prince Gong was always in attendance.

Reform

After witnessing the horrors of the Opium Wars and Taiping Rebellion that had destroyed much of China's economy, Cixi was convinced that the country needed reform. Above all, she believed that it was necessary to modernise the military along Western lines.

As part of what is known as 'Tongzhi Restoration', or 'Self-Strengthening Movement', Cixi ordered that Europeans be appointed to lead and train the Chinese Army and Navy. She was careful, however, not to have too many foreign soldiers on Chinese soil, particularly in the interior of the country. She also commissioned the building of munitions factories and by 1866 a modern naval fleet was launched.

Apart from military reforms, China desperately needed a modern communications network that included roads, a railroad and telegraph system. While the telegraph was generally welcomed, there was great resistance to a railroad on the grounds that such a vast engineering project would upset the balance of nature. Even worse, the construction of railway lines would disturb the tombs of the ancestors. Even Cixi, who was devoutly religious and held strong Confucian values, felt uncomfortable about such desecration.

The policies put in place by Cixi, as well as the appointment of Prince Gong, were welcomed by the Western powers. But Cixi faced opposition from conservative members of the Court. Her greatest critic was Prince Chun, younger brother of Prince Gong and husband of her sister. Prince Chun was opposed to opening up China to Western trade. After the humiliation of the Unequal Treaties, he was consumed with a desire for revenge against Britain. He even went so far as to instigate local riots against foreigners on the streets of Beijing and Shanghai.

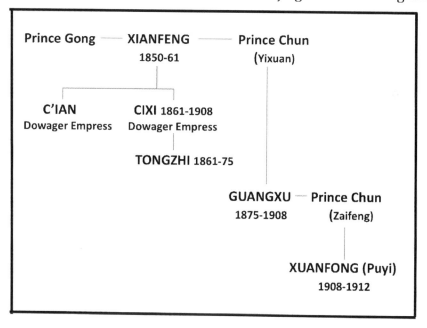

The Tongzhi Emperor

While the two Dowager Empresses were ruling on behalf of the young Emperor Tongzhi, the boy was undergoing an intensive education. His classes began at 5am and he was often still asleep when he was carried in his litter through the dark corridors of the Forbidden City to his classroom.

Cixi chose the best tutors available, whose remit was to prepare the young Emperor for the day when he would come to rule in his own right. She carefully monitored his progress and was concerned to hear that he was often bored and disinterested in his studies.

In 1873, when Tongzhi reached the age of 16, he became the ninth Emperor of the Qing Dynasty and the Dowager Empresses chose two consorts for the young man. The first consort, known as Lady Alute, became the Empress and Dowager Empresses Cixi and C'ian returned to the harem.

Tongzhi was tall and good-looking but he had no interest in government affairs and left all decisions to his ministers. Consequently, Cixi's modernisation programme ground to a halt.

Neither was he interested in Lady Alute or any of his official concubines, preferring instead the company of eunuchs and prostitutes. It was a lifestyle that was incompatible with the strict rules of the Forbidden City and he would often sneak out in disguise at night to visit the city's twilight district.

It was in this context that Tongzhi decided to rebuild the Summer Palace that had been burned down by the British at the end of the Opium Wars. He announced that the palace was needed as a suitable retirement home for the Dowager Empresses. Many speculated that the renovated Summer Palace, free from the restrictions of the Forbidden City, was preferred by the Emperor since it was more suited to his lifestyle.

In 1874, Tongzhi contracted smallpox and the following year, when he was just 18, he died. In line with ancient Chinese tradition, Lady Alute followed her husband to death by ending her own life by voluntary starvation.

The premature death of Tongzhi immediately plunged the Empire into a succession crisis. Having no heir, Tongzhi indicated just before his death that he would leave the choice of successor to the Dowager Empresses. They chose the four-year old son of Prince Chun who was then adopted by Ci'an and Cixi and given the imperial name Guangxu Emperor.

Since Guangxu was under age, the Dowager Empresses resumed their role as co-Regents. Ci'an took the title 'Mother Empress, Empress Dowager' and Cixi 'Holy Mother, Empress Dowager'. In 1881, when Guangxu was just nine, Ci'an unexpectedly died, leaving Cixi as sole Regent.

Between 1881 and 1888, Cixi signed treaties with several neighbouring powers, all of which settled borders that have largely remained in force to this day. Apart from Russia, a treaty with France in 1885 fixed the border with Vietnam. Further treaties with Britain settled the border with Burma in 1886 and Sikkim, an area in North-East India bordering Tibet and Nepal, in 1888.

Through her open-door policy, Cixi managed to double the income of the Empire. She upgraded the army and navy, built shipyards, installed the telegraph and railways, widened the education system and promoted religious tolerance.

In 1889 she decided to retire and hand over to her seventeen-year-old adopted son. The Dowager Empress once more retreated to the harem.

First Sino-Japanese War: 1894-95

While Cixi did her best to bring China's military capability to a level equal to that of the West, her efforts were far outstripped by the attempts of Japan to do the same.

In 1868, Japan had begun a series of political and social reforms known as the 'Meiji Restoration'. Central to the Restoration, also referred to as 'Renovation', or 'Renewal, was the removal of the military dictatorship of the *Shoguns,* and the reinstatement of imperial authority under the Emperor Meiji, who then ruled from 1867 to 1912.

On succeeding to the Imperial Throne, Emperor Meiji immediately adopted an open-door policy. As well as promoting foreign trade, young Japanese were encouraged to travel overseas and learn all they could from the advanced countries of the West.

At the time, Japan believed that the best defence against the threat of rising colonialism, was a strong military. A priority therefore was reform of the armed forces. Compulsory conscription was introduced and both peasants and former *samurai* were recruited to form a united fighting force. Japan also approached the French and German governments for assistance with military hardware, advice and training.

The First Sino-Japanese War was in reality a conflict between Japan and China over Korea. For much of its history, Korea was a virtual vassal state of China while still retaining considerable autonomy. But with the rise of Japan, the balance of power in the region began to shift and Japan cast covetous eyes on Korea.

Korea followed an unusual tradition when it came to succession whereby the King's in-laws chose the succeeding King. In 1864, the 12-year-old Gojong was chosen to succeed King Cheoljong and the regency was placed in the hands of Gojong's father who was known as the Daewongun, a 'generalissimo' type figure. The Daewongun and his advisers were extreme conservatives who advocated an isolationist policy for Korea.

When it came to choosing a wife for the young king, the Daewongun did his best to choose a quiet, unassuming girl as his daughter-in-law. He chose an orphan girl from the Yohung Min clan. She was said to be tall, with beautiful features and a healthy body. Another factor in her favour was that despite being of noble birth, she did not have too many ambitious relatives who could cause trouble at the court.

Unfortunately for the Daewongun, his hopes for an acquiescent consort for his son misfired. Queen Min turned out to be a studious, hardworking young woman who was more interested in politics than palace tea-parties. She appointed her relatives to key positions at court and in 1873 she instigated the retirement of the Daewongun in order that her husband could rule in his own right.

With the fall of the Daewongun, King Gojong, encouraged by Queen Min, was free to adopt a more open-door policy. In September 1875, fearing that Korea would begin trade negotiations with Western nations, Japan took the aggressive action of sending a gunboat, the *Un'yo*, to the Korean island of Ganghwa, scene of previous confrontations between the two countries. Gunfire was exchanged between the Japanese ship and Korean forts. The Japanese retreated, but they remained a threat. They had superior military power and they had proven they were capable of aggressive action. In February 1876, the Koreans were forced to sign the Treaty of Ganghwa.

Under the terms of the Treaty, Korea was recognised as a free and independent state, which was another way of declaring that the country was no longer dependent upon China. Japan and Korea then established diplomatic relations and it was decreed that only Japanese or Chinese would be the diplomatic language between the two countries and not Korean, the language of the people. This was a subtle way of further humiliating the Koreans.

Crucially, the Treaty permitted Japanese vessels unhindered access to Korean waters and Japanese traders were given the freedom to reside and conduct their business anywhere in Korea without restriction.

The most damning part of this 'unequal Treaty', was Japan's right of extraterritoriality, which gave Japanese citizens living in

Korea, immunity from Korean Law. The signing of the Treaty was also a huge humiliation for China in that Korea was removed from China's sphere of influence.

While Queen Min, who was the true power behind the Korean throne, was vehemently anti-Japanese, her father-in-law, the Daewongun, now in retirement, actively supported the Japanese.

In order to counter Japanese influence, Queen Min looked to both China and Russia as potential trade partners and political allies. Consequently, Japan increasingly saw Queen Min as an obstacle to their plans for Korea.

In June 1894, a peasant revolution broke out in Korea known as the Donghak Rebellion. King Gojong appealed to China for troops to help to put down the rebelliion. In response the Qing sent 2,800 troops across the border into Korea. This angered the Japanese and they responded by sending 8,000 of their own troops into Korea.

On the 23rd July 1894, Japanese troops occupied Seoul, captured King Gojong and set up a new pro-Japanese puppet government. Two days later, despite efforts at mediation by the British, open warfare broke out. On the 1st August war was officially declared between Japan and China.

Japan had several advantages over China. She had command of the seas and superior military power as well as extra Korean troops recruited through the newly formed pro-Japanese Korean government.

By the 10th October 1894, Japanese troops had reached Manchuria, and on the 21st November, they had taken Port Arthur. By March 1895, the Japanese fleet was in command of the coastal approach to Beijing, capital city of the Qing Empire.

Faced with imminent defeat, the Qing Government was forced to sign the Peace Treaty of Shimonoeseki.

Treaty of Shimonoeseki: April 1895

Under the terms of the Treaty, Korea was given full independence. Taiwan, the Penghu Islands and the Liaodong Peninsula were all ceded to Japan. However, the Triple Intervention of Russia, France and Germany immediately insisted that Japan relinquish her claim on the Liaodong Peninsula in return for a large financial settlement. This reflected the fact that the Western powers all had their own designs on the region. Tsar Nicholas of Russia, for example coveted Port Arthur as a potential 'ice-free' port, a plan that was supported by his cousin Kaiser Wilhelm II of Germany.

China's war indemnity to Japan amounted to the equivalent of some $5 billion in today's currency. Japan was also given trading rights equal to those of the Western powers.

The Korean Queen Min, with her anti-Japanese views was suspected of allying with China and Russia. Consequently, in October 1895, the Japanese orchestrated her assassination. It was an act that received widespread condemnation not only from China but also from many Western countries.

Following the death of his wife, King Gojong and the Crown Prince sought refuge at the Russian Legation. In October 1897, King Gojong proclaimed the founding of the Great Korean Empire with himself as Emperor Gwangmu. This marked complete independence for Korea, ending centuries as a Chinese vassal state.

The Boxer Rebellion: 1899-1901

Under the terms of the Treaty of Shimonoeseki, China lost not only Korea but also large swathes of Northern China. Seen as another 'Unequal Treaty', in addition to those that had ended the Opium Wars, it was further humiliation for China.

An immediate effect of these Treaties was an increase in foreign embassies and Protestant missionary organisations. Embassies, together with families and staff, from eleven different countries settled in an area of Beijing, close to the Forbidden City. Known as the Legation Quarter, it was an area approximately two miles long and one mile wide.

The increasing presence of foreigners and especially missionaries led to a growing anti-foreign and anti-Christian sentiment among a population that was already highly critical of the Imperial Government. A severe drought in 1898, followed by flooding, in the Northern Shandong Province, provoked riots across the region.

Initially small groups targeted isolated churches, sometimes murdering missionaries and Chinese Christians. One such group was the 'Big Swords Society', that murdered two German Catholic missionaries.

Eventually the various disparate groups of rioters united under the banner of 'The Militia United in Righteousness'. They were known in the West as the Boxers, reflecting their practice of Chinese martial arts, or Chinese Boxing. They believed they had right on their side and that their mystical powers, granted by the Mandate of Heaven, protected them from death.

Consequently, the Boxers fought ferociously, facing cannon fire without fear. By June 1890, they were approaching the Legation Quarter of Beijing. As they marched through the streets they called on the people to support the Qing Government and kill all foreigners.

At the time, the Empress Dowager Cixi was officially in retirement, but because the Guangxu Emperor was still an inexperienced teenager, Cixi was the effective ruler. Initially she did not get involved in the Boxer affair but with the threat of foreign intervention on behalf of the Legations, she felt compelled to support the Boxers. On the 21st June 1900, despite some resistance from members of her government, Cixi issued an Imperial Decree declaring war on the foreign powers.

Immediately, a total of around 900 foreign diplomats, civilians and foreign military, as well as almost 3,000 Chinese Christians, were confined to the area of the Legation Quarter where they were held under siege for 55 days. A second, simultaneous, siege took place at the North Cathedral, the main Catholic church in the Xicheng district of Beijing where some 30 priests and nuns as well as a further 3,000 Chinese Christians were trapped.

By the end of July news reached the Legation Quarter that an allied force was approaching Beijing from Tianjin. Known as the Eight Nation Alliance, the force comprised troops from Japan, Russia, Great Britain, France, United States, Germany, Italy and Hungary. With over 20,000 troops, the Japanese provided the largest number of soldiers, while Great Britain sent the largest number of marines. In total, the allied force comprised 54 warships, almost 5,000 marines and around 52,000 soldiers.

At around 3am on the 14th August the Russians were the first to arrive at one of the gates of the legations. Other contingencies followed and by 4pm on the same day the siege of the legations was over.

The combined casualties among the foreign legations and allied forces was 60 killed and just over 200 injured. The losses sustained by the Qing forces and Boxer rebels is unknown but thought to be extremely heavy.

The Boxer Protocol: 7th September 1901

Early on the morning of the 15th August, Cixi, together with the Emperor and members of the Court, slipped out of the Forbidden City in disguise and made their way by cart to Xi'an. It was a long and uncomfortable journey and the royal entourage relied on the hospitality of local farmers and villagers for food and lodging along the way.

Foreign troops then occupied the city of Beijing. In the guise of rooting out any remaining Boxers, an unknown number of innocent Chinese were killed as well as hundreds of Boxers and Qing soldiers who were executed. Reports of atrocities committed against the Chinese population were widespread.

The troops then went on a looting spree across the city but although they seized large amounts of silver and treasures from temples, the buildings, included the palaces, were left untouched.

On the 7th September 1901, Empress Dowager Cixi agreed to the signing of the Boxer Protocol, considered by the Chinese to be one more 'unequal Treaty'. As well as the Eight Nation Alliance, further signatories included Belgium, Spain and the Netherlands.

Under the terms of the Treaty, China was to pay £67 million at the exchange rate of the time, in war indemnity to the eight nations. Although this was to be paid over a period of 39 years, much of the indemnity was subsequently remitted by different nations in the context of the First World War. The indemnity payable to Germany, for example, was remitted when Germany became an enemy of the Allies.

The Boxer Protocol also specified that no Chinese citizen would be permitted to live in the Legation Quarter and foreigners were granted exemption from Chinese Law. China was also forbidden the importation of arms for a period of two years.

Cixi's Final Years

In January 1902, the Empress Dowager, the Guangxu Emperor and the court returned to Beijing. Part of the journey was taken on board a 21-carriage train and people lined the streets to watch the royal procession travel from Beijing Railway Station to the Forbidden City. This was the first time that the Emperor and Dowager Empress had been seen by citizens of Beijing in public and many of the foreigners from the Legations were invited to view the procession from a special building.

Cixi realised that if the Qing dynasty was to survive, she needed to reform the military along the lines of the Japanese *Meiji* Restoration. She sent students to Japan and also to Europe to gain military expertise and she also increased the number of Western civilians in her civil service. She came to rely more heavily, for example, on Robert Hart, the British Inspector-General of the Chinese Maritime Customs Service, who held the post from 1863 to 1911.

Other reforms included the founding of a state bank and a national currency. The most drastic of all her reforms, however, was to begin the process of turning China into a constitutional monarchy.

In an attempt to engage with the West on a more personal level, Cixi invited wives from the Legations to the Forbidden City for tea and she also employed Western educated Chinese on her personal staff in the palace.

On the 14th November 1908, the Guangxu Emperor died after a short spell of 'stomach ache'. For several years he had been under virtual house arrest for his suspected involvement in a coup. In 2008, a hundred years after his death, forensic tests revealed that the level of arsenic in his remains were 2,000 times higher than normal. This confirmed what many at the time had suspected: that the Guangxu Emperor had been poisoned.

Cixi immediately named his successor as the Xuantong Emperor. He was the two-years-old nephew of the Guangxu Emperor and became known as Puyi. Cixi died the following day, on the 15th November, 1908.

Within a few short years, on the 12th February 1912, the Xuantong Emperor was forced to abdicate, marking the end of the Qing Dynasty and the end of Imperial China.

Conclusion

During the 52 years between the end of the Opium Wars in 1860 and the collapse of the Qing Dynasty in 1912, China was forced into signing further 'Unequal Treaties' so adding to her century of humiliation.

Throughout this period, the Qing Empire was effectively ruled by Dowager Empress Cixi during the regency of two child emperors. Even when the Tongzhi Emperor and Guangxu Emperors came of age, Cixi continued to influence policy from the confines of the harem.

Cixi's greatest challenge was to steer the country towards modernisation and to a more open-door policy in the face of resistance from the conservative elements in her government.

She believed in containment rather than expansion. Her sole aim was to secure the unity of the Empire. Between 1881 and 1888 she signed treaties fixing the border with Russia, with France regarding the border with Vietnam and with Britain setting the border with Burma.

In the 19th Century, China faced humiliation at the hands of the Western powers during the Opium Wars. In the 20th Century, Japan's aggressive expansionist policies under the *Meiji* dynasty, proved to be her greatest threat.

Despite the fact that Cixi had commissioned Western expertise to help in the recruitment and training of the Chinese military, as well as having created a modern navy, China's forces were no match for the Japanese. Consequently, when China and Japan went to war over Korea, a defeated China was forced into signing another humiliating unequal treaty.

Under the Shimonoeseki Treaty of 1895 China finally lost Korea as a vassal state, as well as Taiwan, the Penghu Islands and the Liaodong Peninsula.

The Boxer Protocol that followed the Boxer Rebellion in 1901 marked the final humiliation for the Qing Dynasty. Under the terms of the Protocol, China was committed to the payment of immense war reparations. But the most humiliating clause gave foreign powers, including Japan, the right to live in the Legation Quarter, an area denied to Chinese citizens. Furthermore, it gave all foreigners in the Quarter immunity from Chinese Law.

Historians and analysts have commonly blamed Cixi for the disasters that befell China during this period. She has been criticised for spending too much money on the rebuilding of the Summer Palace when the money was needed for the armed forces. She has been blamed for defeat at the hands of Japan by adopting a policy of appeasement. She has also been accused of holding back modernisation and refusing to adopt an open-door policy with regard to trade.

However, in her book *Empress Dowager Cixi: The Concubine Who Launched Modern China*, Jung Chang paints a different picture. She presents Cixi as an enlightened ruler who consistently worked towards reform and modernisation. The truth probably lies somewhere in the middle, but it is quite likely that being a woman she would have had enemies within the conservative faction of the Court who would have criticised her despite her many achievements.

According to Jung Chang, Cixi admitted having made two major mistakes. First was her untimely spending on the Summer Palace, but perhaps more seriously was her alliance with the Boxers against the foreign powers. It was probably with the intention of making amends for the latter, that she put so much effort, after her return to Beijing, into wooing the ladies of the Legation.

What is undeniable, however, is that while she may not have been highly educated, she was a woman of steely reserve, immense stamina and an unparalleled sense of duty.

Following the devastation of the Boxer Rebellion, the Legation Quarter of Beijing was completely rebuilt. Apart from being home to the Foreign Embassies, the Quarter began to attract tourists, artists and writers from across the globe. They wanted to see for themselves this ancient country that had been a mystery for millennia.

After thousands of years of dynastic rule, Imperial China was ebbing away. A new, modern, China was being born.

*****

CHAPTER EIGHT

Republican China

During the decades leading up to death of Cixi in 1908, numerous revolutionary groups were springing up, both in China and among Chinese dissidents living in exile. Some of these groups believed that China's problems could be solved through reform. Others sought the downfall of Cixi and reinstatement of her adopted son, the Emperor Guangxu.

A more dangerous element believed that the only solution to China's problems was the complete overthrow of the Manchu Qing Dynasty, if necessary by force, in favour of a Republic.

Sun Yat-sen, who later became a contender for Republican China's first Provisional President, came into this latter group. In 1905 he formed the *Tongmengui,* also known as the Chinese Revolutionary Alliance.

Another celebrated revolutionary, who joined Sun Yat-sen, was the young female writer and dissident Qui Jin. After studying in Japan, she fought hard for women's rights, particularly against the practice of foot binding and oppressive marriages. Being an outspoken critic of the Qing, on the 12th July 1907, she was finally arrested. A few days later, she was publicly beheaded in her home village. She was just thirty-one. Today Qui Jin is considered a national heroine and her life has been portrayed in many plays, films and books.

1908	Death of Cixi, Child Puyi enthroned as Xuantong Emperor
1911	Xinhai Revolution, overthrow of Qing Dynasty
1927	Start of Civil War
1931	Japanese invasion of Manchuria
1932	Puyi installed as 'Emperor of Manchukuo'
1934	The Long March
1937	Japanese invasion of China
1945	End of World War II, Resumption of Civil War Kuomintang move to Taiwan as Republic of China
1949	Declaration of People's Republic of China with capital in Beijing

The Xinhai Revolution: 1911

The catalyst for revolution came with the Wuchang Uprising on the 10th October 1911, a day that is now celebrated as China's National Day.

With an increasing number of foreign legations trading across the country, the need for good rail connections with the coastal cities led to a flourishing of railroad building, usually financed by individual provinces. However, when the Qing government threatened to nationalise the railways in order to pay off the national debt, a resistance movement known as the Railway Protection Movement was formed.

In October 1911, members of this resistance movement in the Wuchang District of Hubei Province joined with members of the Chinese Revolutionary Alliance in a planned uprising. On the 10th October the revolutionaries were also joined by members of the New Army. The mutineers seized the Qing garrison and eventually took control of the city of Wuchang.

On the 11th October the mutineers set up a military government for the province of Hubei and by the end of December a further eighteen provinces had fallen into the hands of the revolutionaries.

Yuan Shikai

Following the First Sino-Japanese War of 1894-95, China's various provincial armies were united as the New Army, also known as the Beiyang Army. The New Army came under the leadership of General Yuan Shikai who was also a senior government official.

Yuan Shikai had been very much involved in Cixi's reform programme. He was responsible for abolishing the Confucian examination system and replacing it with the Japanese *Meiji* system of education.

More crucially, Yuan Shikai led the negotiations that resulted in the abdication of the six-year old child Emperor Puyi on the 12th February 1912. In return for his efforts, he was offered the post of first Provisional President of the new Republic of China. Sun Yat-sen, leader of the Revolutionary Alliance had been the favoured contender for the post, but since the Revolutionaries were militarily weak, Sun Yat-sen withdrew his candidature.

Yuan Shikai held ambitions beyond that of Provisional President and in December 1915 he claimed the title Emperor of China. It proved to be an unpopular move with the people and after just eighty-six days as 'Emperor' he reverted to being Provisional President. Yuan Shikai died three months later at the age of 56.

The next few decades would be marked by feuding between various military 'warlords' within the New Army. Known as the 'Warlord Era' it lasted from 1916 to 1927, when Chiang Kai-shek, following the death of Sun Yat-sen, finally succeeded in uniting the waring forces under the Kuomintang.

The 'Emperor' in a cage

The story of the last Emperor of China is portrayed in the acclaimed 1987 film 'The Last Emperor', directed by Bernado

Bertolucci and based on Puyi's autobiography and filmed on location in the Forbidden City. Although extremely well received, especially in the West, the film does have its critics. For example, a review in the Guardian Newspaper, dated 16th April 2009, by Alex von Tunzelmann, claims that while the film is a fairly accurate portrayal of the political history of China, it gives a romanticised view of Puyi's personal life.

Tunzelmann suggests that while Puyi's sexuality might have been in question, there was no doubting his extremely cruel treatment of those around him, and especially the eunuchs, a fact that is glossed over in the film.

The film reveals how the young Emperor became a virtual prisoner in the Forbidden City following his abdication in February 1912.

But despite having no freedom, Puyi retained his Imperial title together with the right to be treated with royal dignity. The document, 'The Articles of Favourable Treatment of the Great Qing Emperor After His Abdication', dated 26th December 1914, laid down eight main clauses regarding the status of the Emperor following his abdication.

Under the terms of the Articles, the Emperor was to receive an annual subsidy equivalent to a maximum of $4,000,000 and he was permitted to retain his personal staff. His personal property was to be placed in the care of the Republic of China and his military guard was to be transferred to the War Office of the Republic.

According to Puyi's autobiography, his life continued much as before. His meals continued to consist of scores of different dishes and he never wore the same clothes twice. Nothing was wasted, however. It had always been the tradition that surplus food and clothing was sold off by the eunuchs, a practice that resulted in widespread corruption.

Over the next twelve years, Puyi remained a prisoner in the Forbidden City while living a life of unparalleled privilege. In 1922, following Qing tradition, he married two wives, one became his Consort, the Empress Wanrong and the other became his First Concubine. The wedding celebration, which was elaborate, was largely paid for by the Revolutionary Government.

Under the tutelage of a Scotsman, Sir Reginald Johnston, Puyi continued his classical studies and also developed an interest in all things European. It is thought that the pro-monarchist faction of the Republican Government had influenced the decision in the appointment of a tutor. It was believed that Johnston, being familiar with a monarchical system, would be the right person to prepare Puyi for a possible return to the throne.

Throughout his confinement, news of the turbulent events erupting across China were largely concealed from the young Emperor. But in 1924, when the warlord Feng Yuxiang seized Beijing, his lifestyle in the gilded cage was abruptly ended.

Feng Yuxiang immediately abolished the special privileges enjoyed by the Emperor under the *Articles of Favourable Treatment* and for the first time Puyi was faced with the reality of his situation. He was forced to leave the Forbidden City with his two wives and he sought refuge at the Japanese Concession in the cosmopolitan coastal city of Tianjin.

Puyi spent six years in Tianjin socialising with British, American, Russian and Japanese expatriates. While he lived the life of a playboy, the Empress became increasingly addicted to opium. She also gave birth to a child, said to be that of a lover. But the child unexpectedly died immediately after the birth while in the care of Japanese medics.

In 1932, a year after the Japanese invasion of Manchuria in 1931, Puyi was installed as 'Emperor' of the new Japanese puppet state of Manchukuo (Manchuria). He had always hoped that one day he would regain his title of Emperor of China and he believed that being Emperor of Manchukuo would be a first step towards his goal.

His hopes were dashed when the Japanese were defeated in 1945 at the end of World War II. Puyi, together with his brother and a handful of faithful servants, was captured by the Russians. He was imprisoned in Siberia for four years and he was generally treated well. Throughout this time, the Russians refused all requests from China to have the Emperor extradited, a decision that probably saved his life. However, in 1949, when the Chinese Communist Party came to power under Mao Zedong, Puyi was repatriated to China.

The last Emperor was fully expecting to be executed on his return to China. Instead he was forced to undertake a ten year 're-education programme' during which time he was forced to watch newsreel footage showing the horrors of the Japanese occupation.

Puyi was finally released by the Communist Government and lived the rest of his life as an ordinary citizen. He was employed in Beijing as a state gardener and in 1962 he married a nurse, Li Shuxian. After just five years, of what might have been the happiest period of his life, he died of natural causes on the 17th October 1967 at the age of 61.

According to an interview given to the Inter Press Service in 1995, the 70 year-old Li Shuxian claimed that a wealthy Hong Kong business man named Zhang Shiyi had offered to bury Puyi's ashes in a new cemetery that he was building close to the ancestral Western Tombs. He also promised to bury Li Shuxian's ashes, as well as those of another of Puyi's concubines, alongside the Emperor.

Puyi's widow died of cancer two years later at the age of 72 and her ashes were buried alongside those of the last Qing Emperor in the new Hualong Imperial Cemetery.

Sun Yat-sen

Following the 1911 Xinhai Revolution that transformed China from a monarchy into a republic, the country splintered into various factions. Members of the Qing government and New Army formed themselves around various 'Warlords', all jostling for power. The other major faction was the Chinese Revolutionary Alliance, also known as the *Tongmenghui* (United League). The Revolutionary Alliance was originally founded in Japan in 1905 by a group of dissidents, led by Sun Yat-sen.

Sun Yat-sen was born in Southern China 1866 and at an early age he was sent to Honolulu to live with his elder brother. When he was ten, he went to Iolani School, which was a private coeducational college run by the Church of Hawaii. While there, he studied British History, mathematics, and science as well as Christianity. He also became proficient in English. When his brother feared that he was becoming too influenced by Christianity, he was sent back to China.

Despite his brother's concerns, Sun was baptized in Hong Kong in 1884 by an American Missionary of the Congregational Church of the United States. He then went on to study medicine at the Guangzhou Boji Hospital under the Christian missionary John Kerr and during this time he attended the Tsai Church that had been founded by the London Missionary Society.

Sun became increasingly frustrated with the conservatism of the Qing government and its refusal to consider adopting more modern Western technology. By 1891, along with other dissidents, he began spreading the idea of overthrowing the Qing. These revolutionary ideas gained momentum following China's humiliating defeat at the hands of the Japanese in 1895.

After a number of failed uprisings, Sun spent several years in exile in Japan, the United States, Canada and Britain, seeking both political support and funding for the revolution. At around the same time, he formed his political philosophy known as the 'Three Principles of the People', incorporating the principles of nationalism, democracy and welfare.

When the Wuchang Uprising and Xinhai Revolution occurred in 1911, Sun was in the United States. On hearing the news, he immediately returned to China. On the 29th December 1911, he was elected Provisional President of the new Republic of China. However, as mentioned above, he later relinquished this provisional post to Yuan Shikai, who had been promised the position on condition that he secured the abdication of the Emperor. Another reason for handing over the Presidency was because at the time, Sun did not have the military backing compared to Yuan.

Kuomintang

Despite having lost the Presidency, Sun Yat-sen was successful in two other areas. First, he was able to unite the various revolutionary groups under a new body known as the Kuomintang. Second, due to his command of English and having travelled in the West, he was able to gain a degree of support from foreign powers and the Chinese diaspora in North America.

The Kuomintang, meaning Chinese Nationalist Party, and often referred to as the KMT, was the successor to the Chinese Revolutionary Alliance (*Tongmengui*), that was founded by Sun in 1905. In August 1912, Sun succeeded in uniting the Revolutionary Alliance with five other revolutionary groups, marking the foundation of the KMT.

The KMT were hard-line anti-monarchists. Many within Yuan Shikai's party, including Yuan himself, were known to be constitutional monarchists and so not surprisingly, tensions between the two groups emerged.

A key member of the founding group was Song Jiaoren, who had been successful in gaining the support of many middle-class landowners and merchants. When Song was assassinated in Shanghai in 1913, the finger of suspicion pointed towards Yuan Shikai.

Sun and other key revolutionaries then spent several years in exile, mainly in Japan. He also visited Europe seeking support, with little success, from socialist organisations. In 1917 he returned to China and restored the Kuomintang, with its government based in Guangdong.

In July 1921, the Chinese Communist Party was founded in Shanghai by a small group of around 50 members of the KMT. Sun then accepted the offer of Vladimir Lenin to help restructure the KTM along the lines of the Communist Party of the Soviet Union. Agents of Comintern, a Communist International organisation charged with spreading communism worldwide, began arriving in China and under the guidance of Mikhail Borodin, a prominent Soviet adviser, a Leninist party structure was formed within the KMT.

The Soviet advisers also helped establish a political institute to train the Chinese in communist propaganda and techniques, and Chinese students were sent to Moscow for further training. Among those who spent time in Moscow was a KMT officer named Chiang Kai-Shek.

It was during this time that Sun's political theory, the 'Three Principles of the People' (nationalism, democracy and people's livelihood) was officially adopted by the Chinese Communist Party.

Chiang Kai-Shek

Sun Yat-sen died on the 12th March, 1925. At the time, the cause of his death was thought to be liver cancer. After a brief power struggle, Chiang Kai-Shek gained control of the Kuomintang.

Chiang was quite a different character to his predecessor. Sun, who had trained as a doctor and converted to Christianity, was a devout revolutionary and vehemently anti-monarchist. He had spent many years in exile and had imbibed Leninist ideology. Chiang had risen through the Qing military and was a devout nationalist who believed in conservative Confucian values.

Another major difference between the two, was that Chiang's experience while undergoing political and military training in Moscow, had convinced him, unlike Sun, that communism would not be suited to China. This belief was to have a profound influence on his later actions.

At the time of Chiang's takeover of the KMT, Northern China was still plagued by the infighting among the Warlords who had seized power in 1916 after the death of Zuan Shikai. Whereas Sun, who was not a military man, had been unsuccessful in bringing the Warlords into the Kuomintang, Chiang was determined to suppress them, if necessary by force, in order to reunite the country.

Initially his plans were thwarted by tensions within the KMT. For example, the left-wing faction, being supportive of socialism, was happy to receive military aid from the Soviets, while the right-wing element, represented by the ideology of Chiang Kai-Shek, was reluctant to get too close to the Soviets because of the fear of the spread of Communism.

An example of this fear of Communism was played out in May 1925, when a group of anti-colonial students demonstrated in front of the Foreign Legation in Shanghai. Sikh police, on the orders of the British, opened fire, killing nine students. A similar demonstration a few days later left another 50 dead. Chiang blamed the disturbances on the Communists and used this opportunity to purge the KMT of many of its Communist leaders by putting them under house arrest. One of those arrested was a young activist named Zhou Enlai, later to become the first Premier of the People's Republic of China.

In July 1926, having removed his most serious opposition, Chiang launched a military offensive, known as the Northern Expedition, against the Warlords and the Beiyang Government. Although the Beiyang Government ruled only part of the country at the time, it was the only official Government of China that was recognised by the international community.

This first offensive against the Warlords came to an end in April 1927 when soldiers from the NRA (National Revolutionary Army) of the KMT, who were opposed to foreign presence in China, attacked the International Settlement in Nanjing. A number of foreign residents were killed and British and American forces responded with firepower from ships moored in the Yangtze River, resulting in the destruction of large parts of the city.

Chiang Kai-Shek once more placed the blame on Communist Party Members who had deserted from the NRA. This time he decided to purge the KMT of all Communists.

On the 9th April 1927, Chiang declared martial law in Shanghai and over the next few days, with the help of an organised crime group known as the 'Green Gang', over 10,000 Communists were arrested and hundreds executed. Thousands went missing. An unknown number managed to conceal their Communist leanings, only to re-emerge some years later. Known as the Shanghai Massacre, or the 'White Terror', the incident is viewed as the beginning of the first stage of the Chinese Civil War.

Chinese Civil War

The Civil War is divided into two phases. The first phase lasted from the Shanghai Massacre in 1927, to 1937, when Japan launched an all-out invasion of China. The two parties in the Civil War then ceased hostilities until the end of World War II, in order to form a united force against the Japanese.

Following the Shanghai Massacre, the KMT split into two political factions, each with its own government. Having expelled all Communists, Chiang formed a new Nationalist Government at Nanjing. He continued to receive foreign support and backing from the West, as well as support from Chinese and foreign businesses.

At the same time, a pro-Communist wing of the KMT formed an alternative Nationalist Government in Wuhan, Central China. In

1931, Mao Zedong, future leader of the Communist Party of China, formed the Chinese Soviet Republic with its capital in Ruijin, in the mountainous region of the south eastern Jiangxi Province.

Consequently, during the early 1930s, China was being ruled by four different interest groups: Chiang Kai-Shek's KMT in Nanjing, an alternative pro-Communist KMT in Wuhan, the Chinese Soviet 'Republic' and different competing warlords.

Events in China reverberated in Russia. Stalin's aim had always been to spread Communism beyond the Soviet Union through the work of the Comintern. Apart from encouraging the work of the Sun Yat-sen University in Moscow, he had been sending Soviet agents to China to support the Chinese Communists working within the KMT. Stalin believed in spreading soviet ideology through the existing governmental system. This was in contrast with his arch-enemy, Leon Trotsky, who advocated that revolution should start with the proletariat by arming the peasantry.

With the collapse of the Communists within the KMT, Stalin withdrew his support from the Chinese nationalists and he concentrated his efforts within the Soviet Union through his policy of 'Socialism in one country'.

From this time on, the official link between Soviet Russia and the Republic of China came to an end, although Soviet agents continued to work with the Communists throughout the period of the Civil War and the early years of the People's Republic of China. Many of these agents were involved in military training and industrial projects. Others were embedded as 'moles' within both the Communist Party and the KMT.

The Long March: October 1934-October 1935

In 1930, Chiang launched a series of offensives against the Communists, known as the Encirclement Campaigns. Mao's newly formed Chinese Workers' and Peasants' Red Army, with

Soviet help, succeeded in defeating the first four of these offensives.

However, by October 1934, KMT troops had encircled the main Communist stronghold of Ruijin. Faced with imminent defeat, the Communists decided to abandon the city and escape through KMT lines with as many troops and civilians as possible.

Zhou Enlai, was put in charge of the logistics of getting hundreds of thousands through enemy lines. The exact date and time of the escape was kept a secret, even from the highest officials, until the very last moment. The exact route to be taken was unclear, apart from the obvious need to avoid KMT forces. The plan was also to aim for the north-eastern region of Shaanxi which was both close to the Soviet border and a Chinese Communist stronghold.

It was agreed that 16,000 troops and civilian administrators should remain behind to act as a rear-guard. Children and the wounded were also left behind, including Mao's own son. While on the march, Mao's wife also gave birth to a daughter, but the child had to be left with villagers. This was the experience of hundreds of women who were separated from their children and later spent years trying to find them, usually in vain.

On the 16th October 1934, 130,000 Communists attempted the breakout. Around 86,000 troops and 11,000 civilians succeeded in getting through, to face an unknown destination and uncertain future. The 16,000 who acted as rear-guard, as well as those who failed to escape, were either killed by the KMT or fled into surrounding countryside.

Considering the strength of the surrounding KMT forces, it is surprising that so many escaped. There is evidence that the neighbouring warlords provided a safe passage for the Communists, but Chang and Halliday in their book, *Mao: The Unknown Story* suggest that Chiang had personal reasons for allowing the Communists to go free.

The authors claim that Chiang Kai-shek's son, Chiang Ching-kuo, was being held hostage at the time in Moscow by the Soviets and that the KMT leader offered to allow the Communists to go free in exchange for the return of his son. Moscow claimed that Chiang Ching-Kuo did not want to return to China. Whatever the truth may be, Chiang spent twelve years in the USSR before returning with his Belarusian wife and child in 1937, some three years after the Long March.

What has become known as the Long March was a serious of marches undertaken by different units of the Red Army, along with an unknown number of civilians. The aim was to escape Chiang's forces in the South and travel to the relative safety of Shaanxi in the Northeast. In order to avoid the KMT, this meant making a detour Westwards before turning North.

The long journey of some 9,000 kilometres (5,600 Miles), was made entirely on foot, across some of China's most difficult mountainous terrain and during a bitterly cold winter. The journey took a year. Only one tenth of the original number completed the journey. In order to survive, the Communists relied on being fed by villagers and in order to replace lost soldiers, due to death or desertion, young men from the countryside were 'encouraged' to join the march.

Mao was often criticised for his harsh treatment of both his own troops and also civilians. In his determination to root out any suspected KMT sympathisers, he frequently used torture. Zhou Enlai was particularly critical of these excesses and although Mao was temporarily demoted, he soon regained power.

Despite the huge loss of life and human suffering, the Long March is seen as a moment of triumph in modern Chinese history. Mao's reputation was soon restored. He had proven himself to be a formidable leader at times of great adversity. He had shown how the strength and determination of the ordinary Chinese people could triumph over imperialist and nationalist forces.

From the isolation of Shaanxi, the Communists were able to consolidate and reform the Party as well as strengthen the Red Army. Perhaps even more importantly, Mao was able to gain further support from the rural workers and peasantry.

Second Sino-Japanese War: 1937-1945

While the official date for the start of the Second Sino-Japanese War is given as 1937, there is a view that the war actually started in 1931 when the Japanese invaded Manchuria. It was at this point that Puyi was installed as Emperor of the puppet state of Manchukuo.

Japan's main reason for invading China was to gain access to her raw materials to make up for a loss of trade resulting from the Great Depression. While the KMT was tied up with the Civil War, Japan took advantage of Chiang's preoccupation with the Communists and began a series of raids across the Manchukuo/Chinese border.

Between 1931 and 1937, tensions increased. Skirmishes, referred to as 'incidents' became commonplace along the

Beijing-Tianjin railway and in 1937 Japan launched a full-scale invasion of the Chinese mainland.

Faced with a common enemy, the KMT and the Communists called a ceasefire and joined forces in the defence of their country.

By the end of 1937, Japan had taken Shanghai and Nanjing, where horrific atrocities were inflicted upon the Chinese civilians. It is reported that Japanese soldiers held competitions to see who could cut off the greatest number of Chinese heads within a set time limit.

During this same period, the Japanese Imperial Army established a human experimentation programme, known as Unit 731, in Harbin, Manchukuo. Between 1935 and the end of World War II, Japanese researchers performed biological and chemical warfare experiments on around 10,300 men, women and children. The majority were Chinese, but the victims also included Soviets, Mongolians and Koreans. Over 3,000 died immediately and an unknown number died within months of the treatment.

The Soviet War Crime Tribunal succeeded in convicting a number of Japanese researchers. But the perpetrators of what were clearly war crimes, were given immunity by the United States in exchange for valuable information on the use of biological weapons.

Although the Japanese succeeded in occupying several major Chinese cities, they were never able to make inroads into the interior. This was partly because of the sheer size of the country and difficulty in maintaining communication lines. Equally, the Communists were able to hold off the Japanese with their guerrilla tactics.

Following a period of stalemate, the Imperial Japanese Navy surprised the world by attacking the US Naval Air Base at Pearl Harbour on the 7th December 1941. This event resulted in America entering World War II in what became known as the

China/Burma/India Theatre of War. In the same year, the Soviet Union invaded Manchuria/Manchukuo.

On the 6th August, 1945, the United States dropped an atomic bomb on the city of Hiroshima in Japan. Three days later another bomb was dropped on the city of Nagasaki. The total number of deaths, which were mainly civilian, from the two bombs, amounted to some 200,000 to 250,000. Over the following months, hundreds of thousands more died from burns and radiation poisoning.

On the 9th August, 1945, the USSR invaded the Japanese puppet state of Manchukuo, as well as inner Mongolia and Northern Korea. The Soviet intervention greatly influenced Japan's decision to capitulate, so ending World War II.

On the 2nd September 1945, Japan signed an Instrument of Surrender in the presence of representatives from China, the Soviet Union, the United States, Britain, France, Canada, the Netherlands, Australia and New Zealand. The signing took place on the deck of the USS Missouri which was anchored in Tokyo Bay.

The Second Sino-Japanese War, which became part of World War II, resulted in the deaths of between 10 and 25 million Chinese civilians, as well as around four million Chinese and Japanese military personnel. It caused the widespread destruction of farmland leading to starvation. The industrial infrastructure of Manchuria collapsed because the Soviets dismantled most of Japan's industrial plant.

The KMT survived the War, but in a much weaker position. The Communists, on the other hand, found themselves in a much stronger position by 1945. They had won the support of thousands of peasants and Communist numbers rose from roughly 100,000 in 1937, to 1.2 million in 1945.

But the conflict between the KMT and the Communists remained and so hostilities resumed in 1945. From a strengthened position, and under the leadership of Mao Zedong, the Communists eventually gained full control of the mainland.

By 1949, thousands of KMT refugees fled to Taiwan where Chiang Kai-Shek established the government of the Republic of China (ROC). On the 1st October, 1949, Mao Zedong founded the People's Republic of China with its capital in Beijing.

The Republic of China in Taiwan was a founding member of the United Nations, but in 1971 the People's Republic of China (PROC) replaced Taiwan as a member state. The Government in Beijing continues to claim sovereignty over Taiwan and declines diplomatic relations with any country that recognises her sovereignty.

Conclusion

The decades between the Xinhai Revolution of 1911 and the founding of the People's Republic of China in 1949, were perhaps the most traumatic in Chinese history to date. During this short period, the Chinese people experienced Revolution, Civil War, Occupation and the consequences of World War II.

Rather than solving the many political and social grievances held against the monarchy, in many ways the fall of the Qing Dynasty opened up even more problems. The most obvious of these was the question of who, or what, should replace Imperial authority. Furthermore, despite the Revolution, many soldiers of the New Army and administrators within the Qing government, remained pro-monarchist under the new Revolutionary Government.

Initially the Kuomintang (KMT), that was founded by Sun Yat-sen, appeared to be the natural successor to the Qing Government and received international recognition. However, when Chiang Kai-Shek became leader of the KMT, the mood changed and the organisation became anti-Communist.

This caused a split in 1927 between right-wing and left-wing elements within the KMT, each with its own government. At the same time, large swathes in the North of the country were still under the rule of competing Warlords.

Throughout the period, the Emperor Puyi was a virtual pawn in the hands of different powers. During his early incarceration in the Forbidden City, rival groups called either for his assassination or for his restoration. In anticipation of the latter, a British Tutor was commissioned to prepare him for a return to the throne at a time when China needed to be open to the West.

Puyi then became a political pawn of the Japanese when he was installed as the puppet Emperor of the 'Manchukuo Empire'. His fate also fell to the Russians, who refused to hand him over to the KMT. And his life was held in the balance when he was passed to the Communists by the Soviets after Mao Zedong came to power in 1949.

At this point Puyi quite expected to suffer the same fate as the Romanov Tsar, but Mao preferred to make him an example to others by putting him through a re-education programme.

Perhaps the most iconic event of the period was the Long March in 1934-35 that took place in the context of the Civil War. Facing some of the most difficult terrain and harshest winter conditions, hundreds of thousands of Communist soldiers and civilians trekked thousands of miles from Jiangxi in the South to Shaanxi in the Northeast in order to escape the KMT.

The Long March is hailed by the Chinese as one of its greatest moments in modern Chinese history. Having proven himself to be a great leader of the people, Mao emerged as a saviour figure. The Long March was also a watershed for the Communist Party with thousands of peasants joining the March as it made its way Northwards.

The Japanese invasion of 1937 brought the two sides of the Civil War together to form a united front in a patriotic defence of their country. However, in 1945, once the World War II was over, the two sides resumed the conflict.

This time the Communists were in a much stronger position and by 1949 Mao had succeeded in defeating the KMT, so uniting the whole country under the People's Republic of China.

Following defeat, Chiang Kai Shek transferred his government to Taipei on the island of Taiwan where the Republic of China (ROC) rules to this day. The status of Taiwan is still disputed between the People's Republic of China (PROC) on the mainland and the Republic of China (ROC) on Taiwan.

What is not in dispute, however, is that the two parties originated as one Nationalistic Republican movement that had been founded by Sun Yat-sen in 1912. Consequently, Sun Yat-sen is considered to be the founding father of modern China and is universally respected by both mainland Chinese and Taiwanese as such.

*****

CHAPTER NINE

Communist China

Mao Zedong

Mao Zedong was born on the 26th December, 1893, in the remote town of Shaoshan in the South-eastern Province of Hunan. He was the eldest son of a relatively wealthy farmer. Mao had a poor relationship with his father, who was a strict disciplinarian, but throughout his life he held a great affection for his mother, who was devout Buddhist.

Although the son of a farmer, Mao showed no interest at all in working on the land. Indeed, throughout his life he was averse to any kind of manual labour, always preferring to read literature of all kinds and later to write his own poetry. The only physical activity that he seemed to enjoy was swimming. He smoked heavily throughout his life and never enjoyed good health.

Mao first attended the local primary school where he quickly became bored with classical Confucian studies. He later went to a more modern school with a Western curriculum and he showed an aptitude for history and geography. He was not good at languages and was never able to throw off his heavy local dialect.

When he was 13, his father arranged for him to marry a girl four years his senior, which was normal for the time. But Mao rejected her as his wife, believing the practice of arranged marriages to be archaic. He later married three times to women of his choice.

Mao opposed the practice of foot-binding and he promoted the equality of women. Both views may have been based on expediency rather than a genuine concern for women's liberation. For example, he expected women to perform manual labour equal to that of a man and in the early years under his leadership, women would only be excused work for a very limited time in order to give birth. There are consequently many reports of women dying in childbirth or losing babies as a result of poor natal care.

It is often said that having witnessed at first hand the suffering of peasants employed by his father, Mao was moved to commit his life to improving their situation. However, Jung Chang and John Halliday, in their book *Mao: The Unknown Story*, claim that there is no evidence that he ever showed any concern for the plight of the peasants, apart from perhaps when it was politically expedient for him to do so.

1949-1976	Mao Zedong Chairman of Communist Party of China
1949-1976	Zhou Enlai 1st Premier of People's Republic of China
1958-1961	Great Leap Forward
1966-1976	Cultural Revolution
1976	Death of Mao Zedong
1976-1981	Hua Guofeng Chairman of Communist Party of China
1981	Trial of Gang of Four
1981-1989	Deng Xiaoping Paramount Leader of Peoples Republic of China
1989	Tiananmen Square Protests

Rise to Power

The account of Mao's rise through the ranks of the Communist Party is fraught with controversy. For example, he was brutal towards both civilians and his peasant armies and he intentionally side-lined the Chinese Communist Party headquarters in Shanghai, while currying favour with Soviet Party headquarters in Moscow. What is unquestionable, however, is that he was ambitious, unscrupulous and a master of opportunism.

Following the Shanghai Massacre in 1927, Mao abandoned the pro-Communist faction within the KMT in Wuhang and set up his own Hunan Soviet in the mountainous bandit region of Jinggangshan. From this remote area, with no telegraph or telephone lines and therefore beyond the reach of Shanghai, he conducted a rigorous recruitment campaign. Peasants were 'encouraged' to join his nascent Red Army. Those who refused had their land seized or were publicly tortured or executed as an example of what could happen to anyone who refused to join the fight against the nationalist enemy.

Because he had no military experience, Mao recruited the help of Zhu De, a warlord who had originally trained at the Yunnan Military Academy and joined the Beiyang Army during the final years of the Qing dynasty. In 1925, Zhu was sponsored by Zhou Enlai for admission to the Chinese Communist Party. In 1928 he marched his army of 10,000 men to the Jinggangshan mountains where he joined Mao. Their joint armies became known as the Zhu-Mao.

Mao made many enemies during his rise to power. He frustrated those at the Chinese Communist Party Headquarters in Shanghai with his maverick behaviour. He intimidated and humiliated his colleagues. But his greatest enemies were those who had suffered torture, if not on his direct order, then by his complicity. Some of his victims complained to the Headquarters at Shanghai. Reports of his behaviour were then passed on to Moscow in the hope of discrediting him.

However, at this time Joseph Stalin was in power as the General Secretary of the Communist Party of the Soviet Union and he supported Mao's actions as being necessary on the basis that individuals are expendable if the Party was to succeed. To make matters even worse, Stalin forwarded the reports to Mao so that he could take the necessary action against the complainants.

With such backing from Moscow, Mao's position was now secure. His actions would go unchallenged and he continued to gain power until 1943, when he became Chairman of the Communist Party of China.

The Korean War: 1950-1953

On the 1st December, 1949, Mao proclaimed the foundation of the People's Republic of China (PROC) as a one-party socialist state.

The following year, at the request of Moscow, he sent the People's Volunteer Army across the border into Korea. Throughout World War II, Japan had occupied Korea, but when Japan was defeated by the Allies, Korea was divided between North and South at the 38th parallel. The North then came under the occupation of the Soviet Union and the South under the United States.

In 1950, Moscow and Kim Il-sung, leader of North Korea, accused the United States of sending troops northwards across the 38th parallel. At the same time, the United States accused the North Koreans and the Chinese, of crossing the line southwards, with the intention of reuniting the Korean Peninsula. The result was a three-year conflict known as the Korean War. In reality it was a proxy war fought on Korean soil. Both China and Russia needed Korea as a buffer state against Japan. The US and her allies wanted a buffer state against Communist China and Russia.

Throughout the war, Mao conducted troop movements from mainland China, while Zhou Enlai commanded the army at the front. The war ended in stalemate and is unresolved to this day.

Land Reform

Soon after the establishment of the PROC, Mao ordered that a land redistribution programme be put in place. Under this policy land was seized from the landowners and given to peasants and landless workers. This applied to all landowners, from the wealthy, with vast amount of land, to the poorest peasant with a tiny plot. Ironically, this would originally have included Mao's own family who had been wealthy landowners.

Unlike the Soviet system under Stalin, whereby landlords were coerced by the State, Mao insisted that that the peasants and workers should seize the land themselves, if necessary by force. He believed that if the peasants murdered and tortured others with their own hands, rather than look on as bystanders, they would be more likely to 'own' the policy, so ensuring a greater commitment to the Party.

Great Leap Forward: 1958-1962

In 1958, Mao introduced the Great Leap Forward, which was an economic and social plan aimed at transforming China from a backward agrarian economy into a nuclear world power. His method was to be a rapid industrialisation programme together with the collectivisation of farmlands.

There was some debate among Party leaders regarding the actual implementation. Moderates believed that industrialisation should precede collectivisation so that farmers would have the equipment necessary for farming on a large scale. Mao insisted that collectivisation was necessary as a first step. In this way, following the example of Stalin's Five-Year Plan, produce from collective farms could be sold off or exported in order to finance industrialisation. Mao's proposal was adopted.

Mao had started the process of collectivisation when he first introduced land redistribution in 1949. At that time, groups of between five and ten farmers were brought together to share their land and tools. In 1953, the number grew to twenty to forty households. In 1956 'higher co-operatives' of between one hundred to three hundred households were formed.

By 1958, all private ownership of land was banned. At the same time, all religious practices, weddings, funerals and festivals were outlawed and replaced by mass propaganda meetings.

Anyone found in breach of the ruling was severely punished or even executed.

The first year of the agricultural programme was reasonably successful in terms of produce, largely due to favourable weather conditions. However, overall, it failed. Peasants lacked equipment and were inexperienced in large scale farming. Often seeds were planted too closely together, leading to crop failure.

The people were also burdened by heavy taxation and at the same time forced to buy State produce at exorbitant prices. An unreasonable production quota was set for each commune and cadres, or militia, were brutal in ensuring that quotas were achieved.

Farms also faced a shortage of manpower because peasants were often transferred to the cities to work in factories. This left an undue burden on the women and children who were left behind. In particular, many older women with bound feed, suffered agony while being forced to work in the fields.

Whereas in previous centuries peasants were able to supplement their income with opium production, this was now banned in favour of grain. In the past, peasants had also been able to move to another region to escape poor harvests and crop failure, but under Mao, any such movement was forbidden.

Mao's agricultural programme under the Great Leap Forward resulted in the elimination of ninety percent the landlord class. It led to between 30 and 55 million deaths due to famine alone and has been described as the greatest famine in history.

Mao presented the outside world with the illusion that China was overflowing with food reserves: that there was plenty for export and also to supply, without cost to countries such as Albania. When the truth gradually came to light, both Canada and Australia offered food aid, even agreeing to send it in secretly in order save Mao's face. But the aid was refused.

When Mao introduced the Great Leap Forward in 1958, he stated that within fifteen years, China would have overtaken the United Kingdom in steel production. In order to do this, he needed money. He borrowed vast amounts from the USSR and he sold off most of China's food to Eastern Europe, Africa and Cuba, despite the fact that the Chinese population starved.

But the urban factories were still not able to produce sufficient iron and steel and so he encouraged the population to set up 'backyard furnaces' in order to supplement production. Once more, unrealistic quotas were imposed on villages and communes. People were eventually forced to burn their own furniture to keep the furnaces working and peasants often slaved well into the night in order to fulfil quotas.

By 1961, it was becoming clear that the Great Leap Forward was not working. People were starving and population growth was in decline. Between thirty and forty percent of homes had been destroyed to make way for factories, community centres, new roads, or simply as a punishment for disobedience.

Several senior Party officials who had visited their home towns and witnessed for themselves the great suffering of the people, began to criticise Mao's policies. In January 1962, at the 'Conference of Seven Thousand', that was attended by 7,000 Party delegates in Beijing, Mao was openly criticised by Liu Shaoqi, Vice Chairman of the Party.

On the last day of the Conference, Mao was forced into a public 'self-criticism', which was common practice throughout the period of the Great Leap Forward and later Cultural Revolution. Consequently, all his agricultural and industrial policies were reversed.

While Zhou Enlai and Deng Xiaoping, who later became *de facto* leader of the People's Republic of China, worked on reversing the country's economy, Mao retreated from front line politics.

At about the same time, China's relationship with the USSR was deteriorating. In 1956, Nikita Khrushchev had openly denounced Joseph Stalin. This led to a process of de-Stalinization and a condemnation of Stalin's policies. Consequently, China and the USSR began to follow a different interpretation of Marxist-Leninism. In 1961, Mao accused the Soviets of revisionism, in other words, a 'revision' of original Marxist-Leninist philosophy. This resulted in political relations between the two powers.

While the USSR moved towards rapprochement with the West, China turned inwards under the leadership of Chairman Mao. China's estrangement from the USSR also gave Mao the opportunity to promote a Marxist-Leninism that he believed would be compatible with China's particular situation.

It was during this period that some of his speeches, covering some twenty-five topics, were published as 'Quotations from Chairman Mao', better known as 'The Little Red Book'. The aim of the book was to promote and preserve Chinese Communism, in other words, 'Maoism'.

The Cultural Revolution: 1966-1976

After four years in relative seclusion, Mao emerged in 1966 with a plan aimed at purging the Communist Party of China (CPC) of all traces of revisionist thought that he suspected was seeping into the Party from Moscow. He was also determined to purge the country of all capitalist tendencies, as well as elitism, by destroying its culture and tradition. He believed that the 'Four Olds' (old customs, old culture, old habits and old ideas) were incompatible with Chinese Communism.

Mao's fourth wife, Jiang Qing, an ex-actress with no political experience, was made Deputy Director of the Central Cultural Revolution Group. This was the body appointed to mastermind the destruction of China's cultural heritage.

Mao had many scores to settle with Party members at the highest level and he felt particularly vengeful towards those who had humiliated him in any way. The first victim to fall was the respected historian Wu Han who wrote a play called '*Hai Rui Dismissed from Office*'. The play tells the story of a Ming dynasty mandarin who dared to criticise a corrupt Emperor. This was construed by many as an anti-Mao allegory with Mao as the emperor. Although Wu Han denied that the play was in any way anti-revolutionary, he was arrested and died in prison in 1969.

A primary aim of the Cultural Revolution was to change the mindset of the young people away from traditional Confucian values towards egalitarian socialism. The initial target therefore became all educational establishments and those who taught in them.

The Red Guard

The plan was for the students, known as the Red Guard, to attack their own schools, universities, teachers and academics. This was a similar strategy to that employed during the Great Leap Forward when peasants were 'encouraged' to carry out 'punishments' on their own neighbours.

The catalyst for the student action, which was also considered to be the start of the Cultural Revolution, was the play '*Hai Rui Dismissed from* Office'.

A group of students from the Tsinghua University Middle School, led by Zhang Chengzhi, and philosophy teacher Nie Yuanzi of Peking University, were pressurised by Mao's wife Jiang Qing to circulate widespread condemnation of Wu Han's play. The situation quickly evolved into a criticism of intellectual elitism in general and big-character posters started to appear across Beijing condemning universities and academics as being counter-revolutionary.

When the university authorities attempted to curb the students, Mao came to their defence. And he went further. Through radio broadcasts and newspaper publications, Mao encouraged the

Guards to continue with their protests. This gave them political legitimacy and the freedom to act without restraint.

Red Guard student groups mushroomed across the country and by June 1966 all classes had been suspended. On the 1st August, 1966 Mao addressed a rally of 800,000 students in Tiananmen Square. At this point the Guards began wearing a red arm band and each student received the 'Little Red Book' which they were expected to carry at all times.

The girls cut their long hair and most of the boys and girls wore loose baggy trousers with a loose tunic caught at the waist by a heavy leather belt. Many wore a peak cap. It was the beginning of the high point in the Mao cult, raising him to an almost divine status.

The students went on a rampage across the country, smashing schools, temples and monuments. They desecrated tombs, including the Cemetery of Confucius and the tomb of the Ming Dynasty Emperor Wanli. They ransacked museums, smashing valuable artefacts and destroying ancient scrolls.

The anarchy quickly descended into violence against people. The first to suffer were teachers and professors. At minimum the teachers faced public humiliation. They would be dragged onto the street and forced into self-criticism in front of jeering crowds. They were often beaten by rods or leather belts or suffered other forms of cruel torture. Others were made to sweep the streets. The violence spread to anyone who was suspected of counter-revolutionary tendencies.

Although some members of the Party, such as Zhou Enlai, expressed concern, Mao instructed the Police not to interfere. The only restriction imposed on the Red Guard was that they should not enter the Forbidden City or any Party building.

By the end of September 1966, almost 2,000 people had been killed by the Red Guard in Beijing alone. In Shanghai, over 700 people committed suicide and more than 500 died.

The violence then moved from the schools and universities in the cities and spread into towns and rural areas across the country. Thousands of innocent people were tortured and often died on suspicion of being anti-revolutionary or simply being related to those thought to be guilty.

Eventually there were signs of conflict within the ranks of the Red Guard. Different factions emerged, each holding to its own interpretation of Mao's often obscure quotations from the Little Red Book.

As anarchy spread, the People's Liberation Army (PLA) voiced concern that the Northern border with Russia was becoming destabilised at a time when Sino-Russian relations were at a low ebb. Faced with a potential Soviet invasion, Mao gave instructions to the PLA to suppress the more radical groups of students.

By February 1967, it was decided that the Red Guard had served its purpose as a tool of the Cultural Revolution. The students were ordered to return to their schools and colleges. Any resistance resulted in a swift, and often brutal, response from the PLA. Hundreds of thousands of young people were sent to the rural areas to undergo re-education programmes.

Despite being outlawed in 1968, disparate groups of students continued to terrorise remote parts of the country until 1979, two years after the end of the Cultural Revolution.

The Gang of Four

Throughout his life, Mao had been a heavy smoker and he enjoyed his drink. It is also believed that in his later years he was suffering from a form of moto-neurones disease and he was almost blind with cataracts. In 1976 he had two serious heart attacks which finally led to his death, on the 9th September 1976, at the age of 82.

As Mao's health declined, power struggles behind the scenes increased. Traditionally, those who posed most threat to the

Chairman's authority were usually purged, an example being Liu Shaoqi who was purged in 1968 for criticising Mao at a Party conference. After suffering public beatings, Liu died in prison the following year. He was posthumously rehabilitated by Deng Xiaoping in 1980 and in November 2018, President Xi Jinping delivered a speech commemorating Liu's life.

Perhaps Mao's most loyal supporter was Lin Biao who had held many senior posts in both the military and the Party. Lin had taken part in the Chinese Civil War and played a key role in the Cultural Revolution. In 1966, he became the First Vice-Chairman of the Central Committee of the CPC, a post that effectively made him Mao's successor.

By 1970, Mao sensed that Lin was becoming too powerful. In order to discredit him, Mao accused Lin of encouraging excessive brutality during the Cultural Revolution. When Mao demanded that Lin make a self-criticism, he refused, which was an affront to the Chairman. Shortly afterwards Lin disappeared from public life. Chang and Halliday, in their book, *Mao: The Unknown Story*, claim that at this point Lin was plotting to assassinate the Chairman. Whatever the truth may be, Lin's body, together with that of his wife and son, were found in Mongolia at the scene of an aircraft accident. His death has been subject of debate ever since.

With the death of Lin Biao, who had been Mao's named successor, Zhou Enlai succeeded as First Vice Chairman and held the post until his death, due to cancer in 1976. Zhou was mourned across the country and hundreds of thousands packed into Tiananmen Squire on the day of the funeral. By then Mao just had a few months to live but was able to nominate Hua Guofeng, a relatively unknown politician, but a loyal supporter, as his successor. Hua then became Chairman of the CPC. While not a natural leader, he was a pragmatist. He reopened the universities and introduced entrance examinations that attracted around seven million students.

Those who fought for power prior to Mao's death could be divided into two groups. Lin Biao (before his death), Zhou Enlai and Hua Guofeng made up an alliance from within the Politburo. Those in the other group, who became known as the Gang of Four, were Mao's wife Jiang Qing; Zhang Qunqiao, a political theorist; Yao Wenyuan, a literary critic and Wang Hongwen, an activist from the labouring class. Apart from Wang, all had a background in the arts and literature and Zhang and Yao could be described as intellectuals.

All four were members of the Central Cultural Revolution Group, the body that was given responsibility for steering the Cultural Revolution. Jiang Qing, with her theatrical background, staged many revolutionary operas; Zhang and especially Yao, who was a literary critic, were involved in the early stages of the Revolution by masterminding the condemnation of the play *Hai Rui Dismissed from Office*.

Throughout the ten-year period of the Cultural Revolution there were tensions between the Establishment, represented by the Politburo, the Army and the Police and the Central Cultural Revolution Group, represented by the Gang of Four. Much of the conflict surrounded disagreements over the excessive use of violence.

When Mao died, the struggle for leadership came to a head. Jiang Qing appeared to show little sorry at the death of her husband and for a few weeks the Gang of Four continued as before. However, at a heated Politburo meeting, Jiang Qing claimed that she was the rightful successor to her husband as Chairman of the Party. But Jiang had made many enemies. She was distrusted by senior Party officials and becoming ever more disliked by the public.

Hua Guofeng, the officially designated successor to Mao, together with other Party officials, plotted against Jiang Qing and her associates. They were all arrested on the 6th October 1976 and spent the next five years in prison.

In 1980, the Gang of Four were brought to trial on charges of 'usurpation of power' and 'anti-Party and anti-socialist' activities. They were also accused of persecuting 750,000 people and causing the death of over 34,000 over a period of ten years between 1966 and 1976.

Jiang and Zhang were sentenced to death, later commuted to life imprisonment, but in 1991 Jiang committed suicide while in custody. Yao and Wang were sentenced to life imprisonment, commuted to 20 years.

While the Gang of Four were undoubtedly guilty of many crimes against the people, they were certainly not the only ones. It is generally considered that they were used as scapegoats for a national crime against the people of China. This avoided putting the blame on Mao and therefore preserving his name for the sake of the CPC.

Deng Xiaoping

Hua Guofeng received the credit for bringing about the downfall of the Gang of Four. He also introduced a moderate programme of reform and made several overseas visits in an attempt to engage with the West. But he was generally thought to be a weak leader and overcautious. He was soon toppled by a more popular, and stronger, Deng Xiaoping. However, unlike in previous decades under Mao, Hua was not purged nor did he suffer any physical harm. He was simply demoted to a lower rank.

Deng Xiaoping was born in 1904 into a peasant family from the province of Sichuan. When he was 15, he travelled with a group of 80 students to France to take part in a five-year work-study programme. It was in France that Deng joined the Communist Party and first met Zhou Enlai. Deng later studied at Sun Yat-sen University in Moscow where he met Chang Kai-shek's son.

Deng took part in the Long March and the Civil War. While he supported Communist ideology, he was critical of some of Mao's economic policies. Consequently, he was purged and spent between 1966 and 1973 in exile, during which time he was sent to work in a steel factory, where he was able to put to use the skills that he learnt in France. He was purged again briefly for a second time in 1976, when his supporter, Zhou Enlai died.

Mao had been drawn to philosophy, books and poetry. Zhou Enlai's public persona was one of suave sophistication with a flair for languages and a gift for foreign diplomacy. Deng was an administrator with a passion for education, science and technology. He has been described as advocating a 'socialist ideology with free enterprise'.

When Deng became paramount leader of the People's Republic of China in 1978, he reversed many of Mao's policies while maintaining respect for the Chairman. He rehabilitated hundreds of the purged cadres and promoted the resumption of cultural life.

Deng then embarked upon an ambitious programme of market-economy reform. He sought advice from Chinese American scientists and sent a five-week delegation on a fact-finding tour of Europe, visiting many factories and ports. He also encouraged closer ties with Japan and other SE Asian countries.

In 1979, Deng went on an official visit to the United States with his wife, who was a physicist in her own right. They visited the Johnson Space Centre and the Boeing site in Seattle. In 1980, he met with Margaret Thatcher and discussed the return of Hong Kong to mainland China. The outcome was the signing of the Sino-British Joint Declaration committing the return of Hong Kong to China by 1997. At around the same time, Deng acquired a similar declaration from Portugal agreeing the return of Macau by 1999.

Tiananmen Square Protests

Under Deng Xiaoping, China experienced rapid economic growth and social change. While this benefitted a minority, the majority of the population still experienced poverty and rising inflation. The students also had their grievances. They were unhappy with the slow process of reform, the one-party system that restricted political engagement and they demanded more freedom of the press and freedom of speech.

In 1986, Fang Lizhi, an astrophysics professor who had taught at Princeton University in the United States, conducted a lecture tour of Chinese universities. He stressed that without political reform, the country had no chance of becoming a world economy. His lectures inspired the students and protest groups began to spring up. By December 1986, demonstrations against the government were taking place in all the major cities.

Student unrest gained momentum throughout the following two years. At the same time, similar protests calling for political reform were spreading across Eastern European countries. Demonstrations became commonplace and increasingly violent as protestors clashed with the army and police. On the 20th March, 1989, martial law was declared.

Events came to a head on the 1st June 1989, when around one million protestors gathered for Tiananmen Square at the funeral of Hu Yaobang, a prominent pro-reform politician. For four days the students occupied the square and some 300,000 troops were stationed in surrounding streets. Skirmishes between soldiers and students broke out, some proving fatal.

On the 4th June, when the students refused to disperse, the troops were ordered to forcibly clear the square. The world watched live footage as tanks rolled in. The moment was immortalised with an iconic image of a lone man standing defiantly in front of a tank.

The actual number of deaths resulting from the Tiananmen Square Protests, sometimes referred to as the June Fourth Massacre, has been cause of much dispute. Official Chinese Government figures have been put the number at no more than

300 fatalities, but figures acquired from diplomats stationed in Beijing at the time, estimate the number to be in the thousands.

Apart from those killed, hundreds of thousands were injured or arrested. Those Government officials who were accused of mishandling the affair, were dismissed from their posts.

1989 proved to be something of a watershed for China. Since Mao's death in 1976, and especially under Deng Xiaoping, the country had started to enjoy a period of economic growth and social reform, as well as a rapprochement with the West. However, following the Tiananmen Square Protests, certain reforms were reversed, censorship increased and freedom of the press was curtailed. Discussion of the event within China was officially forbidden by the CPC, with only scant mention allowed in official textbooks.

The Tiananmen Square Protests and the way that the Chinese government handled them, caused untold damage to China's image abroad. The European Union and the United States subsequently placed arms embargoes on the country, that remain in place to this day.

Deng's reputation, both within China and on the world stage, suffered. He resigned as chairman of the Central Military Commission in 1989 and for the next few years he kept a low profile.

However, in 1992 he re-emerged and embarked upon a tour of the Southern provinces. He returned to the theme of his original economic plan, stressing the importance of economic growth, the market economy and China's role as a world trade leader.

Deng Xiaoping died on the 19th February, 1997 at the age of 92. His legacy can be encapsulated in what is referred to as the 'Deng Xiaoping Theory' which combines Marxist-Leninism-Maoism with China's socio-economic situation. Crucially, he is considered to be the architect of modern China.

Conclusion

The People's Republic of China was proclaimed on the 1st October, 1949. At the time there was widespread starvation, largely as a result World War II and the Civil War. There was also ongoing political instability due to the conflict between the Nationalists and the Communists.

Mao Zedong was not an obvious leader for the country. He had no military background, no overseas experience, was not an orator and not particularly charismatic. But he had proven himself to be a genius of guerrilla warfare in the fight against the Nationalists. He was ruthless and excelled in opportunism. He was also highly ambitious. Mao's master-card, however, was to win the support of Joseph Stalin.

After Stalin's death in 1953, there was a change in relations between the USSR and China. When Khrushchev succeeded Stalin, he criticised many of Stalin's policies, which led to a process of 'de-Stalinisation'. Mao believed that this was a betrayal of true Marxist-Leninism. He accused Khrushchev of encouraging revisionism and he spent the rest of his life fighting any signs of revisionist thought spreading in China.

Mao's greatest ambition was to turn China into a nuclear world power. Key to achieving this was the need for a rapid industrialisation programme. Although relations with the USSR had cooled at the official level, China continued to receive Soviet technical and financial support throughout the period.

A first part of the Great Leap Forward was a land reform programme that involved the forced collectivisation of farms. The result was the destruction of vast amounts of agriculture, the dismantling of the landlord class and mass starvation. The aim of the programme was to produce food, not for the people, but mostly for export, so bringing in income to finance Mao's industrialisation programme.

Mao built many factories for his rapid industrialisation plan but they failed to produce sufficient steel. Consequently, he ordered that the people should build furnaces in their own backyards to supplement factory production.

The Great Leap Forward was ultimately a failure and the human cost ran into the loss of millions of lives. Mao was forced to accept a degree of responsibility and he retreated from political life for the next few years. It was during this time that he started to formulate his next project; the Cultural Revolution.

In 1966, at the start of the Cultural Revolution, Mao's objective was to eradicate all signs of revisionism, elitism and capitalism. Essentially, he was embarking upon a class war against academics and capitalists. Apart from the human cost, China's religious and cultural heritage was virtually destroyed, to be replaced by Maoism that was encapsulated in his Little Red Book.

In the early stages, the Red Guard students were instrumental in targeting the academic institutions. As they became active more widely, anarchy set in and they were disbanded. The Cultural Revolution continued, however, until Mao's death in 1976.

Throughout Mao's rule, many innocent people had been made scapegoats for crimes against the people. Just before his death, Mao was complicit in accusing The Gang of Four for excessive use of violence.

When Deng Xiaoping succeeded as paramount leader, he reinstated thousands of those who had been purged. He himself had twice been purged for being critical of Mao and so it was no surprise that he began a reversal of Mao's policies. However, he was very careful to avoid criticism of Mao's person, because for much of the population the Chairman was, and to a degree still is, revered by the people. For example, Mao's huge portrait is still displayed at Tiananmen Square.

While Deng Xiaoping's succession was generally welcomed by the West, within China, there were those who believed that he had betrayed Maoism. He also lost some credibility following the

Tiananmen Square Protests in 1989, an event that damaged China's image in the eyes of the world.

Between the fall of the Qing Dynasty in 1912 and the Second Sino-Japanese war in 1937, China struggled with the change from imperialism to republicanism. Between 1949 and 1997, republicanism was replaced by communism.

During this time China experienced political, social and economic upheaval on a monumental scale. At the same time, the country suffered two revolutions; one political and one cultural. And it suffered invasion, civil war and a world war.

In just over eighty years, China made the transition from thousands of years of imperial rule, into a socialist state combined with capitalism. Mao Zedong had forced through the early changes in land ownership. Deng Xiaoping was to be the architect of modern China. Under Xi Jinping, China has become the world's second largest economy and world power.

*****

EPILOGUE

In September, 2018, I visited China. The burning question in my mind at the time was: "how is China managing to reconcile a socialist ideology with a market economy?". Deng Xiaoping was described as 'the architect' of China's transition from pure socialism to 'Socialism with Chinese Characteristics'. Under Xi Jinping, the transition appears to be complete, at least, on the surface.

Xi Jinping, sometimes referred to as the 'paramount leader', is the 7th President of the People's Republic of China. He was born in Beijing in 1953. Xi's father held several senior positions in the National People's Congress but in 1963 he fell victim to one of Mao's purges and was sent to work in a factory. At the time, Xi was just ten.

The whole family suffered during the Cultural Revolution. Xi's secondary education was interrupted when the schools were closed and students forced to humiliate and criticise their teachers. His sister died when the family home was attacked by Red Guards and his mother was forced to publicly denounce his father, who was then imprisoned for four years.

Xi later obtained a Doctor of Law Degree that included topics in revolutionary history as well as law and politics. He joined the Communist Party in 1974 and gradually rose through the ranks until he was appointed to the Politburo Standing Committee in 2007. In November 2012, Xi was elected General Secretary of the Communist Party of China and the following year he was elected President of the People's Republic of China.

When Xi Jinping became General Secretary of the CPC, he announced his signature philosophy, known as the 'Chinese Dream'. He claimed that this 'Dream' would be realised by the end of the 'Two Centenaries', when China would be both materially comfortable and fully developed. The date of the first centenary would be 2021, marking the 100th anniversary of the founding of the Communist Party of China in 1921. The second centenary would be in 2049, marking the 100th anniversary of the founding of the People's Republic of China in 1949.

He called on the youth to "dare to dream", to work hard to fulfil their dreams, to strive with a pioneer spirit in order to revitalise the nation. This has echoes of Mao's call to the youth of the Red Guard at the beginning of the Cultural Revolution.

Xi Jinping's 'Chinese Dream' has also been compared to the 'American Dream'. Xi had spent some time in the United States in 1985 and it has been suggested that he was influenced by that experience.

Both the 'American Dream' and the 'Chinese Dream' stress the importance of the entrepreneurial spirit. But there are differences. While Americans claim to have already achieved world status as the most powerful nation in the world, China sees it as a work in progress, but very much achievable.

Furthermore, the 'American Dream' is based on a philosophy of individualism. Although the 'Chinese Dream' encourages entrepreneurialism, this is very much a collective act, with each individual contributing to China's ongoing transformation. The result is that entrepreneurs in the United States are likely to have far greater freedom than their counterparts in China, who could be subject to restrictions imposed by the State..

On a macro level, the belief that despite outward appearances, the Chinese Government is ultimately in control, is causing tensions between the United States and China. This is currently being played out in relation to China's phone giant Huawei. As the company prepares to launch its ground-breaking foldable 5G phone, the Mate X, concerns are growing that the network system could be used for spying.

Despite Huawei's denial of state involvement, the Company's CFO Meng Wanzhou was arrested in Canada in December 2018. Since then, the Trump Administration has been lobbying allies to reject Huawei's 5G technology.

Isobel Asher Hamilton, in her article *Mike Pompeo is bringing the hammer down on Huawei on his European tour* (*Business Insider,* Feb. 12, 2019), reports Secretary of State, Mike Pompeo as saying that "it was 'more difficult' for the US to partner with nations that didn't distance themselves from Huawei". This is clearly a veiled threat to anyone thinking of working with Huawei.

In a later article (Mar 3 2019), Hamilton writes: *Trump's administration is warning US allies to stay away from a powerful Chinese company – but not everyone's listening'*. She gives a run-down of how allies have reacted: **Britain** is concerned but may still use Huawei 5G; **Germany, India, United Arab Emirates** and **New Zealand** are all likely to use Huawei G5. **Japan** and **Australia** have already banned the Company and **Poland** will probably do the same.

Hamilton concludes, therefore, that perhaps the majority of US allies are ignoring President Trump's rhetoric and are still prepared to trade with Huawei despite concerns of possible espionage. It is also likely that Japan, Australia and Poland would have banned the Company anyway, regardless of warnings from Washington.

Another Chinese initiative that is being watched by the outside world with caution, is the Belt and Road Initiative (BRI). In 2013, Xi Jinping announced that this ambitious project would not only restore the ancient Silk Road, but go much further and connect 60 countries across Asia, Europe, Africa and the Middle East. The plan is for an overland route by both road and rail (the 'Belt') as well as a maritime route (the 'Road') that together will connect all the regions. In relation to the maritime route, the celebrated 15th Century Admiral, Zheng He, is being reinstated and held up as the iconic Chinese mariner.

Xi refers to the $900 billion BRI project as forming a 'Community of Common Destiny'. He envisages a community of nations, starting with Asia and eventually spreading as far as Europe.

While the Chinese may welcome and also benefit from the initiative, some of China's neighbouring countries, many of whom are in debt to China, are perhaps less enthusiastic. For example, small countries such as the Pacific island Republic of Vanuatu worries that any renegotiation of their national debt would be conditional upon joining the BRI, as was the case with Papua New Guinea and Fiji.

Not surprisingly, the West, and particularly the United States, has expressed most concern. The fear is that although the project is being heralded as a technological initiative, it is essentially a means whereby China can spread its particular form of socialism. In response, Australia, Japan and the United States, have formed a trilateral partnership aimed at developing projects in the Indo-Pacific Region to counteract the influence of China. There is also a plan to provide funding to help those countries being targeted by China.

It is interesting to note that the members of this tripartite, Australia, Japan and the United States, have all banned Huawei. This would reinforce the strengthening of an international alliance against China's interests.

At the time of writing, (March 2019) China and the United States are in the middle of a trade war. Although there appears to be no immediate end to the conflict at the moment, there are signs of a softening. President Trump has not increased his rhetoric recently and President Xi seems to be adopting a gentler tone in relation to the BRI. There is even speculation that the two Presidents of the world's greatest powers may meet later this month to discuss trade relations.

Some observers have noted that "As some countries move backwards by erecting 'walls', China is contriving to build bridges, both literal and metaphorical" (*Xinhua*, a Chinese state-run media agency).

This would reinforce my own experience during my recent visit to China. When visiting the Great Wall, our guide was very keen to explain that the Wall, which for millennia was intended to keep foreign enemies out, is now a bridge, opening the country up to the rest of the world. In other words, it is being heralded as a wall of 'friendship'.

Xi Jinping would also appear to be holding out the hand of friendship to Taiwan. Although the status of Taiwan has been in dispute since the end of the Chinese Civil War in 1950, Xi is keen to maintain friendly relations. When he met with the Taiwanese President Ma Ying-jeou in 2015, this was the first time the two sides had come together since the ending of hostilities.

While Xi Jinping has led the country towards considerable economic reform, this has not been matched by political reform. On the contrary, it could be said that there has been a reversal. Under Deng Xiaoping, following the Tiananmen Square Protests, the Party cracked down on any form of political dissent. Under Xi, resistance to political reform is evident at the constitutional level.

In March 2018, the National People's Congress removed term limits for the posts of President and Vice President. Xi Jinping was reappointed President and Wang Qishan was appointed Vice President, both effectively for life.

The same Congress approved the setting up of various central leadership groups, all under the control of Xi. For example, Xi is leader of the Central Leading Group for Internet Security and Information and the Central Leading Group for Military Reform. All this, in addition to his role as General Secretary of the Communist Party of China, President of the People's Republic of China and Chairman of the Central Military Commission. Rather than decentralising power, Xi's policy is one of centralisation with himself at the head.

In this new political climate, religious and political freedom has been curtailed. This is especially the case with the Uyghurs who live in the Xinjiang Uyghur Autonomous Region of Western China. For decades, separatist groups have claimed that the region was not part of China, but was illegally incorporated in 1949 into the newly founded People's Republic of China.

The Government's response to any sign of separatist agitation has been to enforce strict political surveillance. Because the Uyghurs are Muslim, the Chinese authorities are also fearful that Islamic extremism might infiltrate the region.

Ever since the rise of Islamist groups such as ISIS, China's hold on the Uyghurs has tightened. Under Xi Jinping, large camps have been built for the internment of suspects. While the West accuses China of infringing human rights, the PRC claim that the camps are justified. There is evidence that many Uyghurs travelled to Syria to join ISIS. Some are now returning and the camps are needed for the process of 're-education' and are therefore necessary in the fight against Islamic extremism.

The Uyghur situation has drawn criticism from the international community similar to the world's reaction to the Tiananmen Square Protests. There is also evidence that the plight of the Uyghurs is drawing sympathy from fellow Muslims in neighbouring states. Most of these countries are partners in China's Belt and Road Initiative. The Uyghur situation may well influence those Central Asian Islamic countries that have yet to decide whether or not to join the project.

Regardless of criticism from the West, US trade sanctions, or the conflict over China's phone giant Huawei, China's economy continues to grow. As momentum gains, the wheels are turning faster. Perhaps the Chinese people are responding to Xi's call to follow the 'Chinese Dream'. If so, it is possible that the Confucian spirit, that puts so much emphasis on duty and an orderly society, is still alive.

It would seem that the hundred years of humiliation was simply a blip in China's long, and proud, history. The sleeping giant has raised her head and will not be humiliated again.

*****

174

北京—上海

经济舱 餐谱

蚝油牛肉粒饭

或

鸡蛋炸酱面

我们还为您准备了
香茗、咖啡、果饮和软饮供您选择。
如果无法供应您的首选菜式，敬请见谅。

适　用：双月1日-10日
版本号：201907

WHO'S WHO AND WHAT'S WHAT

An Lushan	Military governor and leader of An Lushan rebellion
Cai Lun	Court Official said to have invented paper
Chiang Kai Shek	President of the Republic of China
C'ian	Empress Consort of Qing 1852-61, Empress Dowager 1861-1881
Cixi	Empress Dowager of the Qing 1861-1908
Daji	Wife of Di Xin
Daewongun	Regent of Korea 1863-1873
Daoguang	Qing Emperor: 1820-1850
Di Xin	Last King of Shang Dynasty
Dorgan	Son of Hong Taiji and conqueror of the Ming
Erlitou	Ancient Chinese culture
Fuzu	Son of Emperor Qin
Gaozu	First Emperor of Han
Gojong	King of Korea 1897-1907
Gong	Prince, Regent of Qing Empire: 1861-1865
Goryeo	Korea
Guangxu	Emperor of the Qing 1875-1908
Gun	Prince of Chong, worked on mythical flood
Guo Zixing	Founder of the Red Turbans, 1351
Hanhuang	Ancient tribe
Hequin	Marriage of political alliance

Hongwu	Emperor of the Ming, 1328-1398
Hong Taiji	Son of Nurhaci and Emperor of China
Hong Rengan	Cousin of Hong Xiuguan, Leader of Taiping
Hong Xiuquan	Leader of Taiping Rebellion
Hua Guofeng	Chairman of Communist Party of China, 1976-1981
Huang di	The Yellow Emperor
Huaxia	Ancient Chinese civilisation
Jeidushi	Military governor
Jia	Last King of Xia Dynasty
Jiang Qing	Mao Zedong's fourth wife, member of Gang of Four
Jiang Ziya	Noble of Zhou Dynasty
Kangxi	Qing Emperor: 1662-1722
Khitan	Tribe in Northeast China
Kong Fuzi	Chinese name for Confucius
Kuraltai	Council of Mongol leaders
Kublai Khan	Mongol Emperor of Yuan Dynasty
Lin Biao	Vice Chairman of Central Committee of CPC, 1958-1961
Li Yuan	Founder of the Tang Dynasty 618 AD
Li Si	Chancellor/Prime Minister of Emperor Shi Huang di
Liu Bang	Founder of Han Dynasty with title Emperor Gaozu
Liu Ruyi	Son of Concubine Qi

Liu Shaoqi	2nd Chairman of People's Republic of China, 1959-1968
Liu Ying	Crown Prince and son of Emperor Gaozu
Mao Zedong	Chairman of the Communist Party of China
Matteo Ricci	Jesuit priest/scholar
Min	Queen of Korea 1866-1895
Nurhaci	Tribal chief of the Manchu Aisin Gioro clan
Ongud	Mongolian Christian tribe
Prince Peroz III	Son of Sassanid King Yazdegerd
Princess Pingyang	Daughter of Li Yuan, founder of the Tang Dynasty
Qi	Son of Yu the Great
Qi	Favourite concubine of Emperor Gaozu
Qui Jin	Female writer and dissident
Shang	Ancient Chinese Dynasty 1600-1046 BC
Shennong	Ancient tribe
Shenzong	Emperor of Song 1067-1085 AD
Shi Huang di	Emperor of the Qin Empire
Shiji	*Records of the Grand Historian*
Shun	One of the five Emperor/Deities
Sima Qian	Court Historian c 100 BC
Sima Yan	Founder of the Jin Dynasty 265 AD
Sima Tan	Court Historian c 150 BC
Subatai	General of Genghis Khan
Sun Yat-sen	Founding Father of Republic of China
Tang	First King of Shang Dynasty

Tangut	also known as Western Xia, tribe of Northwest China
Taizu	Emperor of the Song 960-976 AD
Taizu	Emperor of Great Jin 1115-1123 AD
Tongmengui	Chinese Revolutionary Alliance
Tongzhi	Emperor of the Qing 1861-1875
Wanli	Emperor of the Ming 1572 – 1620 AD
Wu Zetian	Founder of the (second) Zhou Dynasty 690 AD
Xia	Chinese Dynast 2070 BC-1600 BC
Xianfeng	Emperor of the Qing: 1850-1861 AD
Xiang	King of Wei, c 296 BC
Xiongnu	Ancient Nomadic tribal people North of China
Xuantong	(Puyi) Emperor of the Qing 1908-1912
Yan Jian	Founder of the Sui Dynasty 581 AD
Yao	One of the five Emperor/Dieties
Ying Zheng	King of the Qin State 247 BC
Yongle Emperor	Emperor of Ming 1402 - 1424
Youxiong	Ancient tribe
Yu the Great	Son of Gun and king of Xia Dynasty
Yuan Shikai	First Provisional President of Republic of China
Zaichun	Son of Emperor Xianfeng, became Tongzhi Emperor
Zheng He	Chinese Naval Admiral 1371-1433
Zhou	Ancient Chinese Dynasty 1600-1046 BC

Zhou Enlai	First Premier of the People's Republic of China
Zhu De	Warlord, General 1986-1976

*****

WORKS REFERRED TO

Admiral Zhen He, Dr Michael Teng, pub Corporate Turnaround Centre, 2014

Autumn in the Heavenly Kingdom, Stephen Platt, pub Atlantic Books, 2012

Empress Dowager Cixi, Jung Chang, pub Vintage

Imperial Twilight, Stephen Platt, pub Atlantic Books, 2018

Mao: The Unknown Story, Jung Chang & Jon Halliday, pub Random House Books

The "China Seas" in world history: A general outline of the role of Chinese and East Asian maritime space from its origins to c. 1800. Journal of Marine and Island Cultures, 2012

The Last Manchu, Autobiography of Henry Pu Yi, Last Emperor of China, pub Skyhorse Publishing, 2010

The Rise and Fall of the Great Powers, Paul Kennedy, pub William Collins, 1988

The Terracotta Army, John Man, pub Bantam Books, 2007

Travels of Marco Polo, Edited Milton Rugoff, pub Signet Classics (1961)

Wild Swans, Jung Chang, pub William Collins, 1991

Zheng He – the Chinese Muslim Admiral by Salh Zaimeche pub Muslim Heritage, foundation for Science Technology and civilisation